SUMMERLAND PENTECOSTAL CHURCH

The Dual-Earner Marriage

Also by Jack and Judith Balswick

*The Family: A Christian Perspective
on the Contemporary Home*

The Dual-Earner Marriage

The Elaborate Balancing Act

Jack and Judith Balswick

Fleming H. Revell
A Division of Baker Book House Co
Grand Rapids, Michigan 49516

Published by Fleming H. Revell
a division of Baker Book House Company
P.O. Box 6287, Grand Rapids, MI 49516-6287

Printed in the United States of America

Library of Congress Cataloging-in-Publication Data

Balswick, Jack O.
    The dual-earner marriage : the elaborate balancing act / Jack
and Judith Balswick.
        p. cm.
    Includes bibliographical references (p.).
    ISBN 0-8007-5530-8
    1. Dual-career families—United States. 2. Work and family—
United States. 3. Marriage—United States. I. Balswick, Judith K. II.
Title.
HQ536.B27   1995
646.7'8—dc20   94-48423

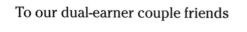

To our dual-earner couple friends

Contents

Acknowledgments

We want to acknowledge the contributions made by our couple friends who have shared with us their struggles and insights on how they have kept their dual-earner marriages alive and well. We also acknowledge the personal and creative touch Greg Hurd added to the manuscript. Debra Sands Miller was a delightful person to collaborate with in the editing, organization, and presentation of our ideas. Our heartfelt appreciation goes to Mary Suggs for her insightful and thorough editing work. Our final thanks go to Floyd Thatcher, who suggested that we write this book, and to Bill Petersen, who nurtured and guided the project from beginning to end. That we have grown together as a couple while writing this book only adds to our enthusiastic belief that a dual-earner marriage can be a fantastically rewarding and fruitful adventure.

Part
1

Laying the Foundation

1

Circuit Overload

They bought a fixer-upper—
the only house on the market George and Gloria Fisher
could afford to buy on their combined salaries. The huge
front yard and magnificent shade trees lent a stately
appearance to the old house, but the house itself had
suffered years of neglect. You name it, the house needed
it—rewiring, replumbing, repainting, recarpeting, and
reroofing.

George and Gloria weren't complaining, mind you; they
were thrilled to finally have a place of their own. Finding
inexpensive innovations, they made their house a comfortable place to raise their three children. The entire
family learned to tolerate inconveniences, but only having one electrical outlet per room was getting to everybody. One day, George came up with a temporary solution. He would place multiple electrical plugs in each
room.

For a few short days he was revered as the family hero. Then all circuits broke loose! Naturally, it was on a weekend. It was just after dinner while the dishwasher was doing its job, the television was entertaining the younger kids, and the computer was helping their teenage daughter finish a report for school. George just happened to plug in his hair dryer so he could train his unruly hair at the same time Gloria plugged in her curling iron. That was the final blow! Circuit overload had occurred. The electrical demands of this family had exceeded the carrying capacity of the old electrical system, and George was left cursing the darkness.

Sometimes, dual-earner marriages are like that old house. Stress overload in a dual-earner marriage can cause problems like circuit overload in an old house. But there are answers for couples in dual-earner marriages, just as there would be answers for George and Gloria Fisher. In this book we share some of those answers with you.

A *dual-earner marriage* is one in which both partners work for pay at least part-time outside of the home. Before the industrial revolution, 90 percent of children grew up with *both* of their parents working in and around the home. Today 60 percent of children grow up with both of their parents working outside of the home. So it is important to address the stress and tensions in the dual-earner family, not only in this generation, but for our children's generation as well.

If your dual-earner marriage is to be successful, you need to put some thought into several important issues:

What do you believe about dual-earner families?
How do you tap into your personal resources?
What can you do to establish quality family and work life?

Coming up with thoughtful answers to these questions is like putting a safe electrical system into your home. It guards against the disasters of overload. It ensures that family members will communicate and cooperate. It encourages each family member to use his or her unique gifts.

Throughout the book, we will share stories from our lives interspersed with stories drawn from the lives of others. We will also draw upon our combined knowledge of psychology and sociology, our experience as marriage and family professors, and our work with numerous people through marriage and family workshops across the country. Our wisdom is also "reality tested," since we've had a dual-earner family for most of our thirty-three years of marriage. Like you, we have struggled with the stresses and tensions that go along with learning how to compose our lives together in harmony. There have been times when we have cursed the darkness and times the stress upon our marriage has caused blowups. But we've gleaned the benefits of coming together in ways that have strengthened our marriage and deepened the level of intimacy in our family relationships.

We learned, sometimes the hard way, how to restructure our lives so we weren't overpowered by the stresses and tensions of the dual-earner family. The focus in the following chapters is on how you as a dual-earner couple can restructure your marriage and maximize the quality of your life.

Internal Strains on the Marriage

Circuit overload is a fitting metaphor for the dual-earner home. Sometimes there isn't enough time to do all that needs doing; so, like George and Gloria Fisher, you are tempted to look for make-do solutions to remedy problems. Members of the modern family are often so engrossed in their own private lives, however, that they are unaware of the drain on family energy. When the family denies there is a problem, members tend to blame each other rather than consider where they plug into the family's overload problem.

Dual-earner parents may unknowingly take shortcuts that endanger the entire system. The marriage then suffers from inadequate energy, and the children suffer from inadequate leadership by the parents. Soon, blown fuses leave everyone in a state of confusion and disarray.

The blowing of temper fuses may provide a temporary release, but it does nothing to alleviate the source of the problem. The unending cycle of blowing and replacing fuses adds to the frustration and is destructive to family relationships. As family members grope in the dark, minor irritations become major issues, and meaningful connections become more and more remote.

When faced with circuit overload, some people knock themselves out with the impossible motto, "just try harder." Most often it's the woman who takes on two full-time jobs—one in the workplace and the other in the home. Her double duty makes her susceptible to the superwoman complex. She makes valiant efforts to get everything done, but just doing the bare necessities takes about all she can manage. In putting the needs of everyone else first, she forgets about the personal toll it takes. Often, the superwoman feels perpetually frustrated and inadequate because she never accomplishes all she sets out to do. Then she blames herself for not being good enough, translating her failures into a personal put-down. Overdoing leads to physical and mental symptoms like fatigue, bodily tension, habits of excess, and depression.

Sometimes the superparent tries to do it all because his or her spouse does very little. When this is the case, unresolved resentment accumulates, which may smolder into a blazing flame of rage toward the less-involved spouse.

External Strains

Some strains on the family are external in origin. Though most people live in dual-earner families, much of society ascribes a negative stigma to such families. The traditional expectation that wives stay home with their children is an ideal that places tension and even guilt on dual-earner families, especially when males and females don't conform to the traditional stereotypes of male and female roles.

When our friend David decided to be a househusband along with his full-time career as a writer, he was unduly criticized by check-out persons in the grocery store, neighbors, and colleagues. He had to explain over and over again that his work with his young children was a priority in his life, even though he was a man. People obviously felt his choice marked him as an inadequate man and a failure in his work.

Strain can also originate from the work situation itself. You may be looked at with suspicion when you turn down a promotion for the good of the family, or you may feel your job is in jeopardy when you need to take time off to care for sick children.

Signs of Circuit Overload

In over 50 percent of marriages in the United States, both husband and wife work outside of the home. This means that the dual-earner marriage is the most com-

mon form of marriage today! When trying to do it all—
working, parenting, and partnering—dual-earner spouses
can expect circuit overload.

The tragedy is that many dual-earner couples fail to
realize the source of their problem until it's too late. Then
tempers may blow, frustration and anger may increase,
conflicts may go unresolved, and marriage and family
relationships may be destroyed.

What are the warning signs? How do you recognize
you are headed for overload? Ask yourself the following questions to determine whether your marriage is
suffering from circuit overload.

> *Can it be time for bed already?* There are never enough
> hours in the day to do everything that needs to be
> done. You find yourself wishing for forty-hour days.
> You may try to stretch out the hours in the day by
> cutting into time needed for sleep or relaxation.
> You may get up early or go to bed late in order to
> accomplish your work. You may wake up in the
> night concerned about the next day's tasks or what
> was left undone the day before, and you may get
> up in the night to do extra work. You're always
> tired.
>
> *Why don't you do your fair share?* You nag your part-
> ner for not doing enough around the house. You are
> frustrated that others don't do household chores
> according to your personal standards. You criticize
> when chores are not done at a certain time and in
> a certain way. You notice whenever something has
> been left undone. You become annoyed when
> things are put off until later, feeling it has to be done
> now. You keep score of who does what and com-
> plain that work is never shared fifty-fifty.
>
> *When was the last time we had a good talk?* Even though
> a concern or problem has been on your mind for a

while, you can't seem to find a time to sit down and talk about it, and you feel the quality of your marital relationship is suffering. You complain that you don't know what your spouse is doing. You each go your own way and have your own activities without checking in with each other. Miscommunication is a regular experience; it's as if you're not in touch with each other frequently enough to ever connect. You sense you're losing your spouse emotionally.

When was the last time we had sex? You don't have a free moment to think about being a sexual person because so much else is going on in your lives. Putting your sexual relationship on hold has become a pattern because you're too busy or too tired to have sex. When you do have sex, you settle for a quick release of sexual tension rather than taking time for warm and intimate lovemaking. The romantic days of your marriage are over, and you spend little time courting each other to keep the spark going. Sexual passion has evaporated, and sex has deteriorated until it has become a routine, maybe even boring activity.

Isn't it your turn? You and your spouse no longer have a sense of partnership in going about the tasks of daily life together. You complain that it's not your turn to do the dishes tonight. Quid pro quo is your motto—you want to make sure it comes out even. You feel you're being taken advantage of if you go the extra mile. You sense a competitive stance in your relationship, and everything becomes an issue—from feeding the dog to taking out the garbage. You want to make sure you get a fair share of the good things in your life.

Why are we arguing again? You never seem to know what the real issue is, even when you are in the middle of one of your recurring, loud shouting matches.

Minor complaints can lead to serious arguments, and the smallest incidents provoke the biggest fights. Your relationship is spotted with numerous unfinished arguments and unresolved issues that you have never squarely addressed.

Was there a time when life felt good? You yearn to go back to a time when life was less complicated and you felt happier. You find yourself reminiscing about the good old days before careers or children (B.C.) when you could sleep in on Saturday mornings, had more relaxed times together as a couple, and the house stayed clean most of the time. In the good old days, you had more control over your life—you could do more together and get more done. You dream of a time when life will be more manageable and you will feel less harried and tense.

If you have asked yourself any of these questions on a regular basis, you, like many other couples in dual-earner marriages, are probably experiencing the kind of extreme stress and overload that threatens to pull you apart.

Even though you may feel baffled and inadequate, it is important to remember that the source of the problem is not personal adequacy or inadequacy! The problem is that you are facing unique pressures and challenges that place increased demands on both you and your spouse.

It is also important to keep in mind that the possibility for change exists. There is hope for even the most beleaguered of marriages. The following chapters give concrete ways in which hope may be nurtured and brought to fruition in a more joyful, intimate, loving dual-earner marriage.

2

Commitment and Forgiveness

The First Two Foundation Stones

It's an understatement to say that marriage is extremely difficult. Statistics indicate that four out of every ten marriages end in divorce, and the evidence is mounting that the divorce rate is even higher in dual-earner marriages. As a dual-earner couple, you need to establish a firm foundation for your marriage—a foundation that can withstand the pressures and meet the challenging conflicts that can cause you to grow apart.

By using four basic principles—commitment, forgiveness, empowerment, and intimacy—you can establish a foundation for your marriage that will help you cope with the pressures and conflicts inherent in the dual-earner reality. The first two of these principles are (1) the covenant principle—extending unconditional commitment to your partner—and (2) the grace principle—offering and accepting forgiveness. (See chapter 3 for a dis-

cussion of empowerment and intimacy.) When you build
the foundation for your marriage using God's model for
relationship, your marriage has the capacity to not only
stand firm, withstanding internal and external pressures,
but to grow and thrive.

The Covenant Principle: Unconditional Commitment

The Bible offers us a powerful model to emulate in our
marriages. In both the Old and New Testaments, we are
presented with a picture of God's unconditional commitment and forgiveness.

In the Old Testament, God's relationship with the chosen people of Israel is based on a covenant, the central
point of which is God's unconditional commitment. This
covenant is first mentioned in Genesis 6:18. Declaring the
intent to destroy all life on earth because of its corrup-
tion, God offers a covenant relationship to Noah: "I will
establish my covenant with you, and you will enter the
ark." God then instructs Noah, "You are to bring into the
ark two of all living creatures, male and female, to keep
them alive with you" (v. 19). When Noah does what God
commanded, God extends the covenant to Noah, his family, and every living creature.

Next, God makes a covenant with Abraham:

> "I am God Almighty; walk before me, and be blameless.
> And I will make my covenant between me and you, and
> will make you exceedingly numerous." Then Abram fell
> on his face; and God said to him, "As for me, this is my
> covenant with you: You shall be the ancestor of a multi-
> tude of nations. . . . I will establish my covenant between
> me and you, and your offspring after you throughout their

generations, for an everlasting covenant, to be God to you and to your offspring after you."

Genesis 17:1–4, 7 NRSV

Abraham's participation in the covenant is spelled out in verse 9: "As for you, you shall keep my covenant, you and your offspring after you throughout their generations." The rest of the chapter describes in detail their part in the agreement. What can we learn about covenant from these two accounts?

First, the covenant was *initiated by God.* Neither Noah nor Abraham requested or expressed a desire for God's action. God established the covenant entirely on his own loving initiative.

Second, the covenant was not a contractual agreement based on negotiation or specifications, but a commitment given by God *without conditions* and regardless of Noah's or Abraham's decision to receive it.

Third, God desired and even *commanded a response* from both Noah and Abraham. God required that they participate in the covenant. Does this make God's offer conditional? Would God retract the offer should they refuse to reciprocate? Absolutely not! The everlasting covenant was offered with no strings attached and was not dependent on the recipients' response.

Whereas the covenant was *unconditional*, the potential benefits or blessings of the covenant were *conditional.* Noah and Abraham had to participate in the covenant in order to receive the covenant blessing. God would not withhold love should they fail to respond, but their willingness to participate in the covenant made it possible for them to benefit from it. In fact, their participation confirmed them as integral participants in God's working out the glorious purposes of the kingdom.

Finally, God extends the covenant beyond Noah and Abraham by including their families for generations to

come. As covenant history unfolds, we see the unconditional nature of God's covenant repeated as the children
of God, Israel, are repeatedly unfaithful in the face of
God's faithfulness throughout the Old Testament. Yet
God, the faithful parent, gives unconditional love to Israel
even while they disobey, continually reaching out to
Israel in forgiveness, picking Israel up as a child, and reconciling Israel so they can be restored to the blessing of
their relationship with God.

The New Testament repeats this message in Jesus. His
life, teachings, ministry, and death are supreme expressions of God's unconditional love. Jesus teaches about this
unconditional love in the story of the prodigal son (see
Luke 15). God, the loving father, welcomes his wayward
son home with open arms and feasting, even after the son
had squandered his inheritance. Jesus demonstrates this
unconditional love in his ministry as he heals the sick, the
lame, the blind, and the sinner. Finally, Jesus expresses
this unconditional love most fully in his death on the cross.

The unconditional nature of God's love is perhaps
most clearly expressed in 1 John 4:12. "This is love: not
that we loved God, but that he loved us." God's love
comes first, inviting you to come to God with no conditions! Once you participate in the covenant by receiving
such love, you are free to receive the blessing—the ability to love others unconditionally as you have been loved.

Covenant as the Foundation for Married Love

Many marriages are based on *conditional* commitments consisting of contracts between the spouses.
While a contractual commitment may seem to ensure the
continuation of love by making each partner's expectations and obligations clear, it fails to offer the necessary
moral strength and unconditional love needed to sustain
a marriage.

In contrast, the covenant principle demands that marriage be based on *mutual, unconditional commitment.* While God's initial covenant is a one-way, unconditional relationship, the desire of God is that the unconditional commitment be reciprocated. This two-way, unconditional relationship is a *mature covenant* of mutual, unconditional commitment. It requires that you return what was initially given freely to you.

Mutual, unconditional commitment is communicated beautifully in John 15:12, "My command is this: Love each other as I have loved you." Love for your spouse and concern for his or her needs take priority over your demands for equality. In your marriage, it requires that you go beyond a mere agreement about equality, expectations, and obligations and extend yourself to consider your spouse more highly than yourself. This may sound outrageous in our day of egalitarian marriages, but it is the extraordinary way of the Bible.

You may wonder how you can keep this biblical directive in the midst of the daily irritations, conflicts, and stresses of a dual-earner marriage. Yet God's covenant includes a blessing: You have been given the Holy Spirit to empower you to live out the directives of the Scriptures in your marriage. When you do, you establish the foundation for your marriage on the model of God's unconditional commitment. This is the first stone in a strong foundation that will allow your dual-earner marriage to resist the pressures that make it susceptible to overload that can pull it apart.

The Grace Principle: Forgive and Be Forgiven

By its very nature, covenant *is* grace—the unmerited love and favor of God toward us. From a human perspective, unconditional love makes no sense apart from grace. We don't deserve to be loved unconditionally, but God loves us anyway. We fall short of God's unmerited love and favor and like Abraham's descendants, we are repeatedly unfaithful.

How can God continue to offer unconditional love when we continue not to merit it? Through forgiveness. God's supreme expression of unconditional love was that he sent Christ to reconcile us to God. "In him we have . . . the forgiveness of sins, in accordance with the riches of God's grace" (Eph. 1:7). God's grace, through the forgiveness we have in Christ, establishes us eternally in God's love.

When you acknowledge and receive forgiveness, you are free to forgive and be forgiven. When you forgive your spouse and are forgiven by your spouse, you create an environment that nurtures your ability to love one another unconditionally.

Andy and Evelyn had been married for five years, during which time Andy's career had advanced rapidly from editorial assistant to managing editor of a daily newspaper. Evelyn had chosen to give up her job as a dietician when their twin daughters were born. However, when the girls entered preschool, Evelyn became eager to return to the workplace and resume her career. Andy was reluctant to support her. He was afraid that changing his schedule to accommodate Evelyn's would jeopardize his career advancement opportunities. As Evelyn continued to express her desire to return to work, Andy realized the unfair advantage he was holding over her. He asked Evelyn to forgive him, and together they worked out a schedule for household and childcare responsibilities. Rather than trying to support their marriage commitment with an outward form—the law—they chose to sustain their marriage with an inward form—grace.

Christ epitomizes the sacrifice involved in forgiveness—giving up your life for another. God extends grace
in an act of self-giving love. When you forgive, you sacrifice yourself, too. You may sacrifice total commitment to
your career, as Andy did, or you may sacrifice your anger
and blame, as Evelyn did. Giving and receiving forgiveness, you create an atmosphere of grace and self-giving
love.

If you view your relationship with God in terms of law
instead of grace, the meaning and joy of being a Christian is lost. The same is true in marriage. Whereas contracts and rigid rules lead to legalism, grace gives freedom to offer yourself sacrificially and to love responsibly.

Is There Ever Room for Law?

Is there any place for law in Christian marriage? Our
answer is influenced by the apostle Paul: "Christ is the
end of the law so that there may be righteousness for
everyone who believes" (Rom. 10:4). It's not that the law
itself is bad—it points the way to God. Since no one is
perfect, however, the law can never be fulfilled. Christ is
the "end of the law" in the sense that he is the perfect fulfillment of the law. We are righteous in Christ not because
we have kept the law, but because our faith in Christ
brings grace and forgiveness when we fail.

Pamela and Chris had been married for less than five
years when they began shopping for their first pet. They
had spent hours discussing what kind of animal to get.
While Pamela was away on a business trip, Chris found
the perfect dog and bought her. When Pamela returned
home, she was furious to find that Chris had not con-
sulted her first. It was days before she would even speak
to him about it. Finally, she told Chris that he had broken an unwritten rule of their marriage: They were to

share in major decisions. She accused him of being thoughtless in not speaking to her first. Chris, while dismayed, said he understood her feelings and explained that he had only wanted to surprise her. He had felt certain that this was exactly the kind of dog she wanted.

As they continued to discuss the conflict, Pamela realized that she had expected this to be a joint decision. She had ideas of finding the perfect pet together and naturally had expected Chris to go along with her plan. She also had visions of this decision bringing them closer together as a couple. Chris realized that his surprise had broken their unspoken agreement and had disregarded her right to have a say in the decision. They both needed to forgive each other and get beyond the legalism that had provoked the conflict over the new dog. Realizing that their marital relationship was more important than any agreement, spoken or unspoken, they took the time to sort through their expectations and offer forgiveness to each other in order to revive the covenant commitment in their relationship.

Our failure to live up to the law points the way to grace. Each of us needs to continually ask God for grace and forgiveness in life, and each of us needs to continually ask and offer forgiveness to each other to keep the marriage focused on the relationship rather than on the rules.

There is a difference between living by the law and living within agreements and rules that express covenant commitment. While the law—the orderly structuring of our daily lives—can never make us righteous or create the unconditional love we are called to share, it can be an expression of our participation in the covenant and our mutual commitment to serve.

Several years ago, Jack attempted an experiment. He decided to rid us of the law—our existing contractual agreements for dividing the household chores—to see if we could have a dual-earner marriage based solely on grace. Up until then, we had lived in agreement about who was responsible for doing which tasks when. But Jack wanted our marriage to be radically Christian so that we could graciously serve each other free from any sense of legalism or obligation. Jack was sure each would notice what needed to be done and gladly do the work as an expression of our servant love. Judy was skeptical but decided to go along with the proposal.

We soon realized we were not even close to the Lord's model of servant love. We tended to slack off from doing the necessary tasks, or we would assume the other partner would do what was needed. The house got messier and conflicts arose over who should have done what when. Judy began to blame Jack for his idealism, and Jack began to accuse Judy of failing in servant love. The breakdown of our "marriage of grace" was swift, and we had to take time to forgive each other and reestablish our covenant commitment.

This little experiment helped us realize that contracts are an important part of the "grace" in a marriage. We found we had to make clear commitments to our covenant love if we were to participate in its blessings.

Recognizing that grace is necessary for covenant love to flourish in a marriage, you also accept the importance of setting up patterns, order, and responsibility in your marital relationship. In reality, much of your daily routine must be lived according to agreed-upon rules, regularity, and order. Contractual agreements are a necessity among fallen creatures such as ourselves. When those agreements fail, as they inevitably do in our less-than-perfect lives, you rely on grace—to forgive and be forgiven—to restore your covenant commitment. In a marriage based on grace, however, the structure (the rules, regularity, order, and roles you assume) will also be flexible enough to meet human needs rather than being rigid, legalistic systems.

Married life is meant to be lived out in an environment of grace instead of law. Marriage that is based on contract or rigid rules focuses on restriction, judgment, and nonacceptance, setting up barriers to marital growth and stability and increasing the pressures on the dual-earner marriage. When your marriage is based on covenant love, you can create an environment of acceptance and forgiveness that nurtures both partners with deeper vulnerability and depth of love.

When you model your marriage on the two biblical principles of covenant and grace, you establish a firm foundation for a stable marriage that can withstand the pressures and conflicts of the dual-earner reality. As you then complete the foundation with the principles of empowerment and intimacy, the blessing of the covenant is yours: a marriage of growing and enduring unconditional love and an atmosphere of grace.

3

Empowerment and Intimacy

Completing the Foundation

When you begin to build the foundation for a marriage relationship on the principles of unconditional commitment (covenant) and forgiveness (grace), each partner's primary concern is how to build up the other in self-giving love. What develops out of the security provided by this covenant love and atmosphere of grace is that spouses gain the freedom to empower each other, providing each spouse the opportunity to develop in all areas and reach his or her full potential.

Power or Empowerment?

The use of power in the marital relationship can be a source of trouble for many couples. Often one spouse gains control by diminishing the other's power, or one spouse will give up power in order to avoid conflict. Given the pressures, stresses, and tendency toward overload in the dual-earner marriage, you may be especially tempted to either increase or decrease your own power in an attempt to make things go more smoothly.

This behavior is consistent with the conventional definition of power: the ability to affect strongly, to control others, or to exert influence over another. When you apply this definition in your marriage, you are bound to erode, not build, the foundation for a marriage that grows together.

Kate and Rick had spent the better part of their early marriage in graduate school—she in psychology, and he in law. When they completed their studies, Kate was offered an unsolicited, prestigious postdoctoral position in the East, and Rick received a high-paying offer from a Seattle law firm. Kate preferred the East Coast, but all his life Rick had wanted to live on the West Coast. They each struggled to get their own way, holding their ground, trying to change the other's mind, yielding nothing. Neither was willing to accede to the other's interests, because each feared losing the potential power represented by their respective job prospects. Finally, when close friends and family members pointed out what was happening between them, the two recognized they were locked in a power struggle.

Rick and Kate had to take time to sort through this first complicated challenge to their dual-earner marriage. Rather than each looking out for his or her own self-interests by wielding power over the other, Kate and Rick opted to redefine the meaning of power in their relationship. When all was said and done, they agreed to accept Kate's postdoctoral position since there were ample opportunities for Rick to find a law position in that community. They would be open to making a move to the West Coast when it was mutually beneficial for both of them.

Kate and Rick chose to follow a biblical model for power, which defines power as *the ability to positively influence another person*. Such a definition places the emphasis on the potential to influence rather than on the actual exercising of power over another person.

Empowerment is the term used to describe this biblical model for power. When you empower your spouse, you actually increase his or her power by affirming inner strengths and potential and encouraging the development of his or her gifts.

Empowerment involves equipping and supporting, building up your spouse to become all he or she was created to be. Empowerment is appreciating the uniqueness of your spouse. It means that you tolerate different ways of being and doing and do not try to force your spouse into a mold. The spouse who empowers respects differences and does not criticize, sees strengths rather than pointing out weaknesses. Empowerment is the active, intentional process of ensuring that your spouse becomes a powerful person of God.

Empowerment is supremely modeled in the life of Jesus Christ, who came to empower us with the Holy Spirit. "I came that they may have life, and have it abundantly" (John 10:10 NRSV). Jesus rejected the idea that power is to wield control over others but affirmed instead that power is love in action: to serve others, to lift up the fallen, to encourage the weak, and to empower the powerless.

Mutual Empowerment

When both spouses apply the principles of covenant and grace—extending unconditional love in an underlying atmosphere of forgiveness—you create the exciting possibility of contributing to your partner's growth through *mutual empowerment*. This means that both spouses positively influence each other in order to increase the personal power of each. Mutual empowerment rejects the idea that servanthood is a one-way street—both spouses must empower each other to versatility and competence in many areas.

Mutual empowerment is essential to each individual's growth within a marriage but also to the growth and stability of the marriage as a whole. Because the dual-earner marriage demands that spouses take on new roles, face new challenges, and stretch beyond personal limitations, it might even be said that mutual empowerment is necessary if your marriage is to survive. Through mutual empowerment you can equip and support each other to take on those new roles.

The practice of mutual empowerment could revolutionize your dual-earner marriage. When you no longer buy into a secular view of power as a commodity in limited supply, you'll be more willing to share all you have with your spouse. The good news for Christians is that the power of God is available in unlimited supply. Galatians 5:22–23 reminds us of the resources we have to offer one another in the Spirit: love, joy, peace, patience, kindness, goodness, faithfulness, gentleness, and self-control. God's resources are inexhaustible!

When you approach your dual-earner marriage with this godly attitude, both you and your spouse have the opportunity to become *interdependent* rather than *independent* of or *dependent* on each other.

Empowering for Interdependence

You and your spouse can empower one another by mutually challenging each other to take risks rather than becoming dependent on the other. Human insecurity may tempt you to keep your spouse dependent on you or to remain dependent on your spouse, but that only creates a counterfeit security. This kind of marital dependency is not love, but *addiction*: I need you to need me so I can feel good when you can't live without me . . . so I'll keep you dependent so I can be secure. Or conversely, I need you so I can feel good, and I can't live without you . . . so I'll stay dependent so I can feel secure.

When two people live in this kind of marriage, neither is growing as an individual, and they often resent each other for their dependency and neediness. Neither one can find a way out, so they take out their frustrations on each other. Covenant love draws people to a mature attachment, free from dependency.

In our early marriage, Jack was dependent on Judy in social situations. Because Judy had a more extroverted personality, it was easy for her to interact with others socially, whereas Jack was a bit awkward and timid around people. Whenever we spent an evening with friends, we understood that Judy would announce our departure to our hosts when we were ready to leave. We perfected a nonverbal communication system so Jack could give Judy subtle signals (eye contact or a glance at his watch) cueing Judy's role. Judy made sure she was alert to Jack's comfort level so the evening would go smoothly.

After a while, Judy began to feel burdened by this role and asked Jack to take more responsibility for himself and his own needs in social relationships. However, Jack continued to rely on Judy socially, getting irritated when Judy failed to pick up his signals or becoming resentful when he couldn't get a word in when people were talking. Jack not only depended on Judy but failed to develop social skills for himself. His ineptness was causing stress and conflict in our relationship.

One evening, while sitting around the dinner table with three other couples, Jack repeatedly gave signals that he was ready to go home. Judy was having a great time, and since she didn't want to leave, she ignored Jack. Finally, after several glances at his watch and a few loud yawns, Jack stretched his leg under the table and gave Judy a gentle kick. At this point, frustrated with the situation, Judy said, "Jack, why are you kicking me?" The conflict was out in the open now. We had a heated discussion in the car on the way home that became the impetus for our practicing empowerment in our marriage. We agreed that Jack would stretch beyond his comfort zone and take responsibility for saying good-bye when he was ready to leave.

Change can be shocking and uncomfortable, but the empowering principle means you need to challenge each other and be challenged to leave your places of security and dependency so that you can grow in new ways. Empowerment draws you to interdependence—a mature attachment, free from dependency.

Lorna and Kevin both worked as sales managers, Kevin in the automotive field and Lorna in fashion merchandising. They had school-age children. In order to advance their careers, each had to put in long hours away from home at certain times of the year—Kevin with new car previews, and Lorna with seasonal fashion-buying trips. They agreed that at these times, one would take over the housework and childcare during the other's absence. Through mutual empowerment, Lorna and Kevin were each eventually able to advance in their respective careers, achieve more job security, and reduce the travel. This increased their interdependence—each was able to contribute more equitably to the marriage, giving each more time with each other and with their children.

You and your spouse might build interdependence directly by sharing a skill expertise, information, or ability with the other. A partner, for instance, could teach the other how to cook, how to manage the finances, how to repair a leaky faucet, how to interact socially, or how to share feelings openly.

Or you might offer indirect support, like Paul did in his dual-earner marriage. Paul agreed to care for the children two nights a week so Anna could attend a six-week training seminar, which would make her eligible for a promotion at work, more valuable as an earner, and would contribute to her personal growth.

When you depend on God's resources and mutually offer your spouse this love in action, you develop your spiritual character. As each spouse builds the other up spiritually, you not only help each other grow as individuals, you also build the spiritual foundation for a mutually empowering, strong, and interdependent marriage.

Intimacy: To Know and Be Known

Marriages founded on covenant, developed through an interaction based on grace, and lived out in mutual empowerment will have great potential for intimacy. Intimacy is the capstone on a biblical foundation for a thriving marriage.

Intimacy with your spouse is one of the most profound of human experiences. To know and be known, to listen and be listened to, to understand and be understood, to care and be cared for, to live together without fear, shame, or secrets—this is intimacy. This is what God desires for your marriage and what God models for you.

Adam and Eve, in their perfect state, stood before each other openly and honestly. We are told that God walked in the Garden in the cool of the day (see Gen. 3:8) and that Adam and Eve were naked before each other and felt no shame (see Gen. 2:25). The intimacy Adam and Eve enjoyed was an ability to be themselves before God and each other without shame or pretense. This is God's ideal relationship between created beings.

God desires to be known. "The Word became flesh and dwelt among us" (John 1:14 NKJV). Jesus came to tabernacle among us; he came to earth to mingle, and God made himself known to us in that immediate, intimate interaction. God models intimacy for us in self-revelation and relationship.

God wants us to know ourselves and be known. We are encouraged to share our deepest thoughts and feelings through prayer; we are told that the Holy Spirit dwells within us and "intercedes for us with groans that words cannot express" (Rom. 8:26). God desires the same for your marriage relationship and invites you and your spouse to disclose yourselves to each other openly and transparently. You need to take the time to communicate—to share your deepest thoughts and feelings with each other. In all the pressure and hurry of your dual-earner marriage, you must make an effort to take time to listen to, understand, and get to know the innermost thoughts and feelings of your spouse. The beauty of intimacy is that you know yourself only as you share yourself. In this way you affirm and participate in the kind of relationship God desired between married partners—the one-flesh union. The connection between you is spiritual, emotional, and physical.

Obstacles to Intimacy

When both partners work, intimacy is often the first thing to go, as Tom and Alayne discovered. After graduating from business school, Tom took several months off to spend time with his children. His wife, Alayne, was already working full-time in her social welfare career. All was going well while Tom was at home attending to the necessary errands and childcare when Alayne was not available, and best of all, Tom and Alayne spent quality time together in the evenings after the children were in bed.

However, when Tom began to work, he was so overcome with his new duties that his time began to manage him. Soon he was spending long hours at the office. He felt ashamed and found himself apologizing nearly every day for being late or for needing Alayne to perform a task that was his agreed-upon responsibility. To make matters worse, they began to spend their precious time alone haggling over how to manage their time and responsibilities. Often they ended the day with unresolved arguments. Their time together and their intimacy were reduced to the point that their marriage was endangered.

Your marriage will become strained and intimacy will vanish if you disappoint, fail, and even betray the person you love the most. If there is a rupture in your dual-earner relationship—when work takes you away from each other or you find yourself becoming more involved with people at work than with your spouse—your relationship needs to be reaffirmed. Confession is essential to restoring intimacy. You must admit your own mistakes and the offense you've taken at your spouse's mistakes.

Tom and Alayne chose to set aside a day without the children to begin to repair the damage to their relationship. They began their time together by both sharing openly the anger and frustration they felt. When each had been heard by the other, they were free to move on.

Tom felt free to confess his failure to keep up his responsibilities and to manage his time in such a way that the marriage and family had his support and participation. Alayne, too, confessed how offended and angry she was at Tom's absence.

Open confrontation and expression of emotions are a necessary part of an intimate encounter. Your capacity to freely and openly communicate your feelings with your spouse is contingent upon trust and commitment—having no fear. John tells us, "God is love. . . . There is no fear in love; but perfect love casts out fear" (1 John 4:16, 18 NKJV). God loves you with a perfect, unconditional love and prompts you to love others the same way—unconditionally. This brings you back to the covenant basis for your marriage relationship: unconditional love, which allows you to freely communicate with your spouse without fearing rejection, criticism, or betrayal.

Jesus modeled this kind of communicative intimacy during his life on earth. Recall how Jesus asked Peter not once, but three times, "Do you love me?" (see John 21:15–19). Jesus gave Peter the opportunity to reaffirm his love and to indicate his willingness to once again be empowered to feed the sheep. Peter, who had denied Jesus three times, needed the reassurance of Jesus' unconditional love and forgiveness.

"Do you love me?" may be the first question you must ask when the pressure and stresses of a dual-earner marriage threaten your intimacy and even the marriage itself. Tom and Alayne answered "yes" and came back to the basic foundation principle—unconditional love. Once their covenant commitment was reaffirmed, the two of them could look for ways to mutually empower each other in a stressful situation in order to reestablish intimacy in their marriage.

Intimacy will not exist in your marital relationship until you are willing to come out of hiding and be vulnerable with each other. If secrets, fear, or shame are present in your marriage, you may be tempted to hide or put on masks and play roles rather than be real with each other. When this happens, you must forgive and be forgiven to find your way back to each other so that renewal and restoration can keep you in intimate contact.

Putting It All Together

If the dual-earner couple is to draw together and not grow apart, it is especially important that marriage be based on the biblical principles of mature covenant— unconditional commitment, forgiveness, mutual empowerment, and intimacy. These four elements are in continual process in a healthy marriage.

Unconditional commitment provides the security necessary for intimacy. Intimacy can lead to a deeper covenant love, which increases forgiveness and grace in the relationship. Grace leads to empowerment, and empowerment results in interdependence that leads us to be more vulnerable, deepening our intimacy. Together these principles establish a strong and stable foundation for our dual-earner marriage.

Your dual-earner marriage needs a strong and stable foundation to face the challenges and demands of your dual-earner roles. When conflicts arise, as they inevitably will, you can return to the eternal basis of marriage— unconditional commitment, forgiveness, mutual empowerment, and intimacy—and rely on it to support and sustain you, enabling you to grow together rather than apart.

Part
2

Weathering the Storms

4

Resolving Conflict Constructively

Conflict may be uncomfortable or frightening, and it may seem like a sure way to damage a marriage, but in fact it can strengthen your marriage. Marriages that grow together are those that successfully resolve conflict.

Whenever we meet a couple who tells us that they never have any conflicts, we assume either they have not been married very long, they don't know each other very well, they don't talk to each other very often, or they are lying. Conflict is a normal part of any marriage relationship.

Although conflict itself is neither good nor bad, the way conflict is handled can be either destructive or constructive to your marriage. Destructive conflict tears down both spouses and closes the door on communication and resolution. Constructive conflict honors each partner's dignity and opens the door to open, honest communication.

Destructive ways of handling conflicts can be both covert (e.g., when you refuse to deal with conflict or deny it exists) and overt (e.g., when the expression of the conflict is damaging to the relationship). The key to successful conflict resolution is to avoid destructive ways of handling conflict and begin to establish constructive ways to manage conflict in your dual-earner marriage.

Covert Destructive Conflict

Dealing with conflict in a *covert* way nearly always involves some form of denial. You may deny, ignore, or refuse to deal with conflict in the marriage by sweeping the unwanted dirt under the rug to give the appearance that the problem has been eliminated. The motto, "out of sight, out of mind," comforts you with the illusion that the conflict is resolved but, unfortunately, does nothing about the problem that brought about the conflict in the first place. In truth, denial does not resolve but only intensifies conflict because you never acknowledge the source of the problem and therefore never "sweep it up."

Displacement

There are several ways spouses can deny conflict. One common way is by *displacement*. An episode of the comic strip "Family Circus" depicted displacement in a series of cartoon frames showing the boss lashing out at the husband at work; the husband coming home and shouting at his wife; the wife scolding her daughter; the daughter

crabbing at her younger brother; the brother bawling out
the dog; and the dog chasing the cat. The conflict is displaced down the line until, finally, the cat catches and eats
a mouse. Displaced conflict ends with a victim receiving
the final blow. Displacement may seem to provide a safe
outlet for strong feelings, but it never resolves the problem at its source.

Disengagement

Another way to deny conflict is by *disengagement*. Imagine this scenario: Jerry gets angry at his wife, storms out
of the house, screeches away in the car, and then returns
two hours later as if nothing had happened. This burst of
anger followed by withdrawal is called disengagement.
Jerry and his wife never talk about what caused the
blowup in the first place and collude together in the cover-
up. When spouses disengage in this way, they deny and
avoid conflict by gingerly sidestepping sensitive, anger-
provoking issues. Disengagement may seem to defuse a
potentially explosive situation, but in fact it is a barrier
to marital growth, leaving the unresolved conflict smol-
dering, possibly leading to an explosive crisis later on.

Disqualification

A more subtle way to deny conflict is by *disqualification*. One spouse may express anger and then quickly discount his or her angry reaction with an alternate expla-
nation. For example, Pat may get angry at her husband,
Dan, for not doing his share of the housekeeping but then
disqualify the legitimacy of her angry feelings by reasoning that she would not have gotten angry if she had slept
better the night before. Rather than admit anger-produc-
ing emotions and face squarely the problems that caused
them, her disqualification tends to cover them up.

Denial of all kinds is destructive not only to the marital relationship—adding stress to an already overloaded system—but to the personal well-being of each spouse. It causes increased frustration and anxiety in the marriage, and can rob one or both partners of the ability to learn and grow from life's challenges.

Overt Destructive Conflict

Denying conflict is at best a barrier to marital growth and at worst destructive to the marital relationship itself. Even more destructive, however, are inappropriate overt expressions of anger when dealing with marital conflict. If you want to preserve a healthy marriage and grow together in your relationship, overt, destructive behaviors must be avoided.

Hitting Below the Belt

How often in a fight have you been hit by or hit your spouse with verbal comments directed toward personal areas of sensitivity? Each of us has emotionally charged issues or sore spots, and in those areas even a mild verbal punch might feel like a shattering blow. Married couples know each other's most sensitive qualities (e.g., overweight, laziness, penny-pinching, rejection, self-esteem, sexual ability, attractiveness). You can use your spouse's sensitive areas as targets for your verbal assaults when you are aiming to injure your partner and are not fighting fair.

Abusive Expressions of Anger

Although anger as an emotion is not judged to be wrong, the wrongful expression of anger is sinful: "Be angry but do not sin; do not let the sun go down on your anger" (Eph. 4:26 NRSV).

Both covert and overt expressions of anger can be sinful. Denying, ignoring, refusing to deal with, or holding in anger allows it to smolder. When you don't acknowledge and deal with the angry feelings within, you can easily end up expressing your anger with resentful, revengeful, or even physically harmful behavior. The admonition not to let the sun go down on your anger honors the reality of our frail humanity—unresolved bitterness and anger can become destructive to yourself and to others. So although it should go without saying, the fact that spousal abuse occurs so frequently necessitates our including this important principle: *Spouses are not to express anger in verbally or physically abusive ways.*

If you fail to address the anger behind the conflict, you may get caught in a cycle of abuse marked by increasing tension that eventually leads to complete withdrawal and separation or physically harmful behaviors. While either of these reactions may seem to resolve conflict for a while, and the abusing spouse may feel some remorse and lament his or her actions, the real issue has not been dealt with. It isn't long before tension begins building once again and negative emotions intensify until an insignificant behavior or event can elicit a major outburst. Until the anger is addressed, a couple can be caught in an abusive cycle that worsens until someone is seriously hurt. If you find yourself in an abusive situation, we advise you to seek professional help immediately.

"Gunnysacking"

In the heat of an argument it can be tempting to reach into the past for old hurts and gripes to throw at your spouse. Some have called this "gunnysacking." When you push down all the anger and frustration rather than dealing with it directly, you eventually end up carrying a bulging gunnysack full of past anger, disappointment, and hurt. It is tempting to unload your sack onto your spouse during a fight. However, the experience of being dumped on in a fight is devastating, and your partner may become wary of any further attempts at con- structive conflict resolution, fearing he or she will be barraged with muck from the bottom of your sack again.

Game Playing

In response to criticism or conflict, one spouse might play the martyr: "I just can't do anything right," or "I guess it's all my fault." Another might try to trick the spouse into doing favors by feigning weakness, inability, or neediness. Some partners like to play the "poor me" or "kick me" game in order to get sympathy or assistance.

The passive-aggressive game is one of the more sub- tle ways to sabotage conflict resolution. You act in a pas- sive-aggressive way when you verbally deny your anger but act out in an indirect manner with your behavior. The goal in this game is to get back at your spouse indirectly through controlling techniques.

Mary was angry with Alvin for leaving the pots and pans to soak until her morning breakfast shift in the kitchen. She was terse in her response to his "good morning," but when he asked her if she was angry about something, she said, "No." That night Mary showed up late for the dinner Alvin had prepared for their guests, claiming she got mixed up and wrote the wrong time on her calendar.

When you cannot deal with the anger openly, no resolution is possible, and anger continues to be acted out in passive ways. The passive-aggressive spouse is capable of wielding a great deal of control in the marriage.

Not Taking the Other Seriously

You or your spouse may display a lack of concern by ridiculing, clowning, or laughing at the other during a discussion. The spouse who uses such tactics gives the message that he or she is not taking the other seriously and that the other's opinion is worthless, stupid, or not worth considering. It is impossible to resolve conflicts when trusting and open communication is undermined in this way.

Labeling and Name-Calling

A sure way to stop all reasonable discussion is to engage in labeling or name-calling. If, in an argument, you call your spouse *stupid, ignorant, silly, dumb, square, childish, spoiled, compulsive, conceited,* or any other derogatory name, you put your spouse in a box from which he or she cannot escape. Labeling is not only disrespectful, but it also terminates any serious engagement in productive conflict resolution.

Triangling

Triangling occurs whenever two people are in disagreement and one or both attempt to bring in a third party to gain an advantage in the argument. For example, if you and your spouse are arguing over an issue and you turn to your daughter and try to get her on your side by saying, "I'm right, aren't I?" you have tried to set up a triangle. This maneuver not only diverts you from working out your marital conflicts, it is also disruptive to your children, who often get pulled into the triangling process.

Blaming and Avoiding Responsibility

"You make me feel so angry!" This familiar response indicates you aren't taking responsibility for your own feelings. When you think about it, this statement gives the other person incredible power to determine how you feel. Only when you can clearly admit to yourself that it's *your* anger will you be able to determine for yourself how you're going to respond to that feeling.

Generally speaking, when you point the finger and make a *you* statement or ask "Why did you do this?" you are attempting to place blame and avoid taking responsibility. It may be that *why* questions do help you understand the other person's point of view, but usually in conflict situations *why* is used as an accusation rather than as an honest inquiry. Very often your spouse does not really know why he or she did a certain thing, and there is really no response that will ever be able to satisfy the one who asks an accusatory *why* question.

Constructive Conflict

The good news is that conflict can be handled constructively. Once you recognize the covert and overt ways conflict is destructive, you can find practical principles to help you establish constructive ways to manage conflict. By developing strategies for resolving conflicts, you will continue to relieve the internal pressures on your dual-earner marriage and begin to establish the kind of communication and conflict-resolution skills that can enhance your marriage and keep you growing together.

In this spirit, you can use the following steps as guidelines for successful conflict resolution.

Step 1: Admit That Conflict Exists

Remember, covert ways of dealing with conflict nearly always involve denial. Before you can resolve conflict in your marriage, you must stop denying, ignoring, or refusing to deal with it and admit that a conflict exists. Once you and your spouse acknowledge conflict, you can take the necessary steps to resolve it.

Step 2: Identify the Issue

What is the conflict really about? Answering this question can be more difficult than you realize. Conflict often involves more than one simple issue, and you and your spouse may disagree about what the real issue is. However, little progress can be made toward resolving conflict until each spouse can define the issue for himself or herself and then agree on it together. When there are multiple issues, or when you can't agree, the initial task is to decide together what to tackle first. Later you can take on the next issue and consider how these complex issues are interrelated.

Step 3: Choose the Right Time and Place

Choose the right time to deal with the conflict. Many conflicts can be resolved when they arise if you and your spouse have time and if emotional intensity does not prevent you from engaging in a reasonable discussion. In many cases, however, you or your spouse may need a cooling-off time before it is possible to proceed in a constructive way. If you or your spouse find this necessary, mutually agree on a time when you will come back together to work on the conflict.

There may be periods during the day when you or your spouse are better able to be alert. For example, we have learned to schedule our conflict discussions during the early evening hours to avoid the early mornings, when Judy is barely functioning, or late nights, when we risk Jack's noninvolvement.

Conflict resolution also needs to take place on neutral territory, where both spouses will be on equal footing. Just as the husband's workshop is a biased place, so is the wife's study.

Make sure you choose a time and place where you will not be interrupted. Discussing conflict in the kitchen while dinner is cooking or while the children are coming in and out for snacks does not promote concentration or resolution.

Step 4: Stick to the Issue

Have you noticed how easy it is to wander all over the place during an argument? You will be more successful in resolving conflicts when you stick to the issue. This can be especially hard when one of you brings up a related issue, but resist the pull to become sidetracked so you can truly concentrate on the issue at hand. Agree ahead of time that if one spouse digresses, the other can simply call "off limits" as a way of keeping the discussion focused. Later, you may want to broaden your discussion, but initially these left-field issues only make it more difficult to resolve the conflict at hand.

Practical Principles for Problem Solving

Successful conflict resolution demands dialogue—listening to each other and expressing yourself so you can understand and be understood by your spouse. To keep this dialogue open, it is helpful to express conflict in a way your spouse can hear without becoming defensive or retaliatory. It's amazing how smoothly a conflict discussion can go if you practice some basic problem-solving principles in your conflict discussions. You and your spouse can help each other be more open, positive, and constructive in your approach to the issues, small and large, that can result in conflict.

Fight Fair

All couples concerned with constructive conflict must learn to fight fair: *No hitting below the belt.* If you find yourself the target for your spouse's verbal assaults on your sensitive areas, you have the right to yell "foul." This is the signal that your spouse is using a destructive and unfair tactic and needs to back off.

A caution is in order for spouses who are too touchy. If you call foul for so many topics that it inhibits your spouse from addressing important issues in the relationship, you need to challenge yourself to be more open to your spouse's legitimate complaints.

It may help if you and your spouse determine ahead of time to discuss a sensitive topic. If you're prepared for the discussion, you might be able to let your guard down a bit. On the other hand, you'll need to trust your spouse to be gentle in his or her approach to you. Perhaps it would be especially helpful to begin such a discussion with a statement such as, "This topic is very difficult for me because . . . ," or, "I tend to get defensive and want to protect myself. I want to hear what you have to say, but I'll need you to say it in a way that doesn't cause me to put up my guard."

Recognize the Abuse Cycle and Get Help

The abuse cycle can begin when conflicts arise but are denied or covered up. Things might be going smoothly for a couple; they may feel close, even romantic. So when conflict does arise, neither spouse wants to disturb the good feelings. As a result, irritations increase, new anger is added to the original source, and the stress of the negative feelings starts to build up. Finally, the couple can take it no longer, and there is a blowup over some small matter, and one spouse may separate from or physically harm the other. This overreaction is fierce, unexpected, and frightening. Neither spouse understands what the real conflicts are because so much has been hidden and denied, and in this state of anger it is hard to figure out all the complexities of the conflict or its real source.

After the explosion, there is remorse—the abusing spouse may ask for forgiveness, bring flowers, and say "I love you." But since the real conflict has not been addressed, the cycle repeats itself. The relationship plateaus; tension begins building; and finally there is another outburst.

If you find yourself caught in this kind of cycle, you need to get help from a counselor or pastor. Unless you have someone help you deal with your conflicts in a safe, constructive environment, anger will keep you in a continuing cycle of relentless abuse.

To avoid getting caught in a circular cycle, you must be aware of and communicate about the conflicts, anger, and irritations in your marriage. Regularly dealing with conflict will help you accept conflict as normal and keep you from denying or hiding the conflict and anger. Open communication can allow you to deal with conflict so it can enhance your relationship and bring a feeling of closeness and unity without the need for a false honeymoon or major explosion.

Leave the Past in the Past

Don't bring old hurts, anger, or frustration into the current conflict. You and your spouse owe it to each other to start with a clean slate. Stay current with issues, addressing conflict when it arises and dealing with your feelings directly and honestly. And practice forgiveness— extend to each other the pardon and forgetfulness God extends to you.

Concerned, Reflective Listening

Practice listening to your spouse. Don't argue or rebut; simply receive what he or she has to say without judgment. Then reflect your spouse's comments and concerns back in your own words so your spouse knows he or she has been heard and understood. This concerned, reflective listening shows respect for your spouse and builds trust and communication between you.

Positive Strokes

Try giving your spouse a positive stroke before launching into a confrontation. A positive stroke is a statement that gives your spouse the benefit of the doubt. You're not assuming a malicious motive for the behavior. This can make it easier for your spouse to hear and respond to your discontent.

Consider this example: Suppose Matt is annoyed because his wife doesn't hang up her towels or pick up her clothes after showering. He could confront her with: "Gini, I'm tired of you throwing towels and dirty clothes all over the bathroom floor. I think you are trying to make my life miserable. Why don't you just shape up!" Or he could give her a positive stroke first: "Gini, you're generally very good at putting your dirty clothes away, except after you shower. I feel so much better toward you when you remember to pick up after you shower." Using a positive stroke allows what could have been a threatening accusation to become grounds for positive discussion and resolution.

The Clear Message

This simple, three-part statement can be helpful for clarifying complaints and keeping dialogue open:

1. *Declare your feelings.* When you tell your spouse how you feel about a situation, you take responsibility for yourself and your feelings, laying a foundation for trust by being honest and demonstrating congruence between your feelings and your words.
2. *State the issue.* What is the source of this strong feeling?
3. *State your desires.* What outcome do you want in this situation?

Joanie and Peter both work full-time, but lately Joanie has had to put in extra hours on the job. They had agreed that Peter would cook weeknights until Joanie's workload diminished, but lately dinner hasn't been ready when Joanie arrived home. Joanie finally confronted Peter using the three-part statement.

"Peter, I'm angry because dinner has not been ready when I get home from work. I thought we'd agreed you would cook dinner while I am working overtime, and I need us to figure out how to solve this problem."

Peter does not have to be defensive or feel blamed—Joanie has not asked him *why* or said *you,* accusing him of being a bad husband or of trying to undermine their marriage with a malicious plot not to have dinner on the table. Rather, she has clearly admitted to herself that she is angry, and determined for herself how to respond to that feeling. As a result, she decided to file a complaint and requested that they work together to find a solution. Peter now has a chance to state his feelings and thoughts about the matter without having to defend or accuse her in return. He can express what he wants and needs to do about the situation as well.

Brainstorming

Take time to brainstorm all possible solutions to the problem. Brainstorming involves generating as many possible solutions as you can without rejecting, selecting, or censoring. This is a valuable exercise because it helps you to get beyond the idea that there is only one solution to a problem. Brainstorming allows spouses to think creatively and come up with numerous possibilities.

You and your spouse can have a relaxed and fun time together composing a list of every idea that comes to you. After you have generated your list of possibilities, take time to give honest feedback about each proposed solution. Ask yourself how realistic it would be to follow through on each of the solutions you've listed. Consider the pros and cons of each suggestion, and then determine what it would take to make a particular solution work. Finally, select the one solution you both agree on, and make a contract about what each of you will do to keep your part of the bargain.

In order for your marriage to grow, you must learn to resolve conflict constructively, avoiding certain practices and cultivating others. By carefully listening to each other and properly expressing yourself you can be sure that you understand and are understood by your spouse. Practicing these few simple tools will open the way for dialogue—the kind of communication that facilitates constructive conflict resolution and enables you to deepen intimacy within your marriage.

5

What's Your Conflict Style?

Some couples follow all of the suggestions about constructive conflict resolution, avoid destructive ways of handling conflict, but still have difficulty resolving conflict because they have different conflict styles. A *conflict style* is the primary mode of relating we resort to when conflict arises. When faced with the stress of conflict, most people either become *withdrawers, winners, compromisers, yielders,* or *resolvers.*

Each conflict style has both advantages and disadvantages and may be more or less appropriate, depending on the situation. None is right or wrong. In fact, when we look at the life of Jesus, we can see that he used every style. There were times when he was a withdrawer, a winner, a compromiser, a yielder, and a resolver.

Your particular conflict style may consist of a mixture of each type, but as you continue to read, try to identify which best describes your particular conflict style. Once you and your spouse identify your particular styles, you can begin to see the advantages and disadvantages of each conflict style for your married life and learn to apply different styles to different conflict situations.

Withdrawers

Withdrawers are reluctant to deal with conflict and often choose to avoid it. The withdrawer feels safe and secure when there is no open conflict and may value peace so highly that he or she simply withdraws when conflict arises. The withdrawer may have grown up in a violent home, where withdrawal became a way to survive that unsafe and frightening reality. While withdrawers may gain a sense of personal control from their style, it can also be very controlling of others. In one sense, they can hold the emotions of the other person hostage by refusing to deal with them out in the open.

Although avoidance was not one of Jesus' dominant modes for conflict resolution, there were times when he did withdraw. When Jesus healed the man with the shriveled hand on the Sabbath, he greatly angered the Pharisees who "plotted how they might kill Jesus" (Matt. 12:14). Jesus could have confronted the Pharisees as he had on other occasions, but instead, when he became aware of their plotting, we are told that "Jesus withdrew from that place" (Matt. 12:15). We are also told in Luke 5:15–16 that as the crowds of people pressed upon Jesus with their needs for healing, "Jesus often withdrew to lonely places and prayed."

During the final hours before his arrest, Jesus anticipated the imminent conflict.

Jesus went out as usual to the Mount of Olives, and his disciples followed him. On reaching the place, he said to them, "Pray that you will not fall into temptation." He withdrew about a stone's throw beyond them, knelt down and prayed.

Luke 22:39–41

Later, Jesus persuaded his disciples not to take up swords against those who were to arrest him (see Luke 22:47–51).

There will be times when you need to withdraw from a conflict with your spouse in order to be able to think more clearly about the issue. Sometimes angry emotions are so high that it is impossible for you to resolve conflict constructively. At these times, it is appropriate to withdraw from the conflict until you are able to discuss the situation dispassionately. It is also appropriate to set aside trivial conflicts for the sake of more pressing matters.

Withdrawing can be destructive, however, if it sends the signal that the withdrawing spouse does not care enough to resolve conflicts. Therefore, the spouse who withdraws needs to be held accountable by the other and must promise to come back and deal with the conflict at some agreed-upon time.

Winners

Winners enjoy a good argument. They are usually quite verbal and capable of challenging another's point of view and explaining their own. Winners have a strong idea that their way is the right way and may not be easily persuaded that another way can also be right. Winners may be driven to win at all costs. But they must remember that if they win at the expense of their marriage relationship, the cost is too high.

At times Jesus acted like a winner.

> Jesus entered the temple area and drove out all who
> were buying and selling there. He overturned the tables
> of the money changers and the benches of those selling
> doves. "It is written," he said to them, "'My house will
> be called a house of prayer,' but you are making it a 'den
> of robbers.'"
>
> Matthew 21:12–13

Jesus did not yield, withdraw, or compromise. He acted because the law of the Lord was being violated. He acted like a winner—authoritatively and decisively claiming a victory for his Father.

If you're a winner, you have strong ideas about principles. You like to debate, and you're good at it. Perhaps your profession requires you to be articulate and promotes arguing your point of view. Teachers, lawyers, and ministers are often winners in this sense.

Two people in such professions may easily adopt this conflict style in their marriage because they are both go-getters—they like the challenge of taking leadership roles and are energized by a competitive situation. They may use the winner style at work and come home expecting to win in the marital relationship too. But the marital relationship is not a win-lose proposition. While the winner characteristics may serve you well outside the home, competition between spouses can escalate rather than decrease conflict and may short-circuit your ability to see your spouse's point of view.

The danger of engaging in a winner's conflict style is that the real issues sometimes get lost in an argument over principles. When this happens, the conflict can degenerate to a personal level, with each partner feeling the need to win the point to save face. If you use the winner conflict style at home, you risk winning the point but losing the relationship in the process.

Compromisers

Compromisers accept the fact that conflicts can be settled best when one is willing to give in order to get. They are willing to let go of a firm position in order to find middle ground. Compromisers are also willing to move in and out of each of the other styles if this will help resolve a conflict. They may sometimes feel they are misunderstood as being wishy-washy, but in fact they have clear values and are not willing to compromise on principles. However, compromisers *are* willing to let others live by their own values rather than convincing them to do otherwise.

We tend not to associate the compromising style of conflict with Jesus. Yet when the Pharisees sought to trap Jesus by asking him if it was right to pay taxes to Caesar, Jesus replied, "Give to Caesar what is Caesar's, and to God what is God's" (Matt. 22:21). Jesus resolved another situation with compromise when he dealt with the woman caught in adultery: "He who is without sin among you, let him throw a stone at her first" (John 8:7 NKJV). In both situations, Jesus gave an unexpected answer to a single-minded question and opened the way for a new alternative.

In the same way, offering a compromise solution in a marital conflict might open the way for new alternatives. Compromise might be the best way to handle conflict when you and your spouse have different opinions or preferences and must reach an immediate decision. Some conflicts are simply managed better with compromise, such as where to vacation or whether to see a play or a movie on Friday night.

However, compromise may not be the best solution for other issues. For example, the Kakimos are planning to move to a new part of the country. Tami wants to live in the heart of the city where they will both work, while

Duane wants to find a piece of acreage in a rural area some distance from the city. To compromise by living in a suburban home would leave both spouses unhappy and dissatisfied. They will need to use creative thought and cooperation to work together toward a solution that will afford both of them the essential advantages they are seeking.

Yielders

Yielders find it easier to give in to the wishes of another rather than to assert their own wishes. Yielders may justify this stance as necessary for the sake of marital harmony. Some may view themselves as martyrs and even glorify their behavior as supremely Christian. Others may yield because they have a poor self-image and don't believe they're worthy of making requests. After yielding, however, they may feel guilty and wish they had spoken up instead.

One thing yielders may fail to understand is that others often feel guilty for taking advantage of them. The yielding spouse may become the doormat, but when the partner starts walking all over him or her, both can lose respect for each other. The spouse often wishes that the yielder would stand up and express what he or she needs, wants, or thinks.

When handled correctly, however, yielding can be a positive conflict style. Jesus' teaching to turn the other cheek (see Matt. 5:39) models a loving stance that takes into account your partner's human failings. You can choose to yield to an ungracious comment in order to de-escalate the conflict and open up new avenues for communication.

In perhaps the greatest conflict Jesus experienced in his life on earth, he yielded himself to be arrested, falsely convicted, and finally crucified (see Matt. 26:47–68;

27:11–50). His example gives hope that something greater can come out of conflict when you yield appropriately to hurts you might experience in a conflict with your spouse in order to promote new life in your marriage.

Resolvers

Resolvers see to it that conflicts are not swept under the rug. They are determined to work hard at making mutual, egalitarian decisions, and feel that most relationship conflict can best be dealt with through collaboration. Resolvers are intensely invested in working through conflicts and may be frustrated when their spouse does not cooperate or have the same amount of determination to settle things. This style can be problematic if the resolver is so bothered by the lack of resolution that he or she pressures the spouse in order to get closure on an issue.

The resolver style works best in long-term, committed relationships. Since the dual-earner couple needs to work hard to make mutual, egalitarian decisions, most relational conflicts can best be dealt with in this style. While requiring a lot of time, effort, and emotional energy, the resolver style has the potential for offering maximum satisfaction and happiness to both partners.

Jesus modeled this style best in his relationship with his disciples. The resurrection is the best example of resolution made by Jesus. He restored the broken relationship between the creation and the Creator. The chasm caused by human sin was not swept under the rug, but dealt with in a decisive, eternal way.

Jesus modeled a resolution style when he relentlessly and patiently explained himself to his disciples who misunderstood his ways. In his interaction with Peter over the painful break of denial, he confronted Peter face to face with the question, "Do you love me?" not once but three times (see John 21:15–17). This intimate, direct query gave Peter the opportunity to make amends and restore their love.

Identifying Your Conflict Styles

Which of these five conflict styles are you most likely to adopt with your spouse? There may be times when you use any one of the five described. Nevertheless, try to identify the *one* style toward which you most naturally gravitate.

Find a time when you and your spouse can have an hour alone together without distractions. Each of you should independently identify your own dominant conflict style. Then share your selections with each other and together reflect on and discuss the following questions:

How did I learn this conflict style?
What do I like about this conflict style?
What do I dislike about this conflict style?
What happens to our relationship when we each get into our respective conflict styles?
What would I like my spouse to do differently?
What would I like to do differently?

As you answer these questions together, you will probably find that your relationship is a unique combination of styles for handling conflict. Most people learn their styles of conflict in their family of origin, usually adopting the style used by the same-sex parent. When you and your spouse combine your learned styles in a marriage, you may find yourselves locked into a conflict resolution pattern that does not work.

Jennifer, a resolver, is married to Mark, a withdrawer. Both work, and Monday morning their young child wakes up with a fever. Either Jennifer or Mark will need to take time off work to stay home with their sick child. Mark begins to make preparations to go to work without consulting Jennifer. He withdraws from the potential conflict by ignoring the situation. Jennifer, wanting to come to a mutually beneficial solution, tries to persuade Mark to resolve the situation. When he doesn't respond, she intensifies her efforts.

This is a common combination: a pursuer married to a distancer. The more the pursuer (resolver, compromiser, or winner) advances, the further away in the relationship the distancer (withdrawer or yielder) moves.

Expanding Your Horizons

The challenge for the dual-earner marriage is for each partner to expand his or her horizons and consider the possibility of using other styles. This involves giving up the tendency to opt for the style that comes naturally.

The spouse who always withdraws or always yields in a marital conflict is perpetuating a condition that makes it very difficult to adequately resolve conflict. Likewise, conflict resolution is likely to be a problem when the pursuer dictates, manipulates, or controls the way conflicts are handled. If you recognize this pattern in your marriage, realize that the pursuer (resolver, compromiser, or winner) will need to give the distancer (withdrawer or yielder) space and time. The distancer, however, must agree to come back and work on the conflict in a timely fashion.

Jennifer may get further if she stops persuading and pursuing in her efforts to use her resolver style. If she is able to relax and let go of the intensity, she may break the pattern of mutual reinforcement that perpetuates the unbalanced styles, and Mark may take more initiative in the process of conflict resolution. If Mark can resist his tendency to ignore problems and withdraw and instead begin to offer solutions for equal participation in the care of their child, Jennifer can let go of being the sole resolver and begin to trust Mark to take more responsibility.

Sometimes both spouses use the same conflict style. If this is true in your marriage, there is a unique chemistry created by the combination of your styles. For example, if both of you are withdrawers, you may have trouble starting to resolve conflict because you habitually practice avoidance and rarely deal with conflicts. If both of you are winners, you may look forward to a good fight, but you may also have difficulty really hearing your partner's point of view. Those of you who practice compromise may be a little better off—at least you talk about your conflicts. But if you both use an accommodating style, there may be many unexpressed personal wishes, opinions, and needs that are not met in your marriage.

If your marriage is stuck in a nonproductive pattern, we urge you not to become discouraged but to do something about it. By identifying your conflict styles, you are in a position to make constructive changes. It can be a challenge to meet your partner halfway, but as you are able to change and adopt styles for resolving conflict, you can move toward a biblical model of conflict resolution.

We believe that the model of constructive conflict resolution is consistent with what the Bible says about how Christians are to handle conflict:

Therefore each of you must put off falsehood and speak truthfully to his neighbor, for we are all members of one body. "In your anger do not sin": Do not let the sun go down while you are still angry. . . . Do not let any unwholesome talk come out of your mouths, but only what is helpful for building others up according to their needs, that it may benefit those who listen.

Ephesians 4:25–26, 29

When there is conflict, we are told to speak truthfully. The direct implication is that Christians will neither withdraw ("Do not let the sun go down while you are still angry") nor become aggressive ("In your anger do not sin. . . . Do not let any unwholesome talk come out of your mouths"). The text lends support to a direct confrontational style that shows concern for self, the other person, and the relationship.

The passage in Ephesians also points toward cooperation as an ideal between Christians: "We are all members of one body." If there is a dominant social process that should be characteristic of the body of Christ, it is high cooperation or collaboration. "The body is a unit, though it is made up of many parts; and though all its parts are many, they form one body" (1 Cor. 12:12). The implication is that all members of the body—and both partners in a marriage—will work together for the good of the body as a whole.

By using practical principles for constructively resolving conflict and by identifying your conflict styles, you can begin to eliminate some of the ways of handling conflict that have caused stress and heightened the tension in your dual-earner marriage. Your marriage can grow as you open new avenues for appropriate confrontation, communication, cooperation, and collaboration.

Part

3

Continual
Challenges

6

Different Script, New Roles

Early in life we are all given gender scripts. As soon as a little boy is old enough to be in the sandbox, he plays with trucks, fire engines, doctor sets, and a variety of other toys that help him imagine a future in which he is the provider and protector. By the time a little girl is barely able to walk and talk, she is given dolls to love and soon after inherits a full complement of toys—dollhouse, miniature kitchen, tea set, dress-up clothes—that help her anticipate her role as homemaker. The message is clear: He will be responsible for making the money; she will take care of the home and children.

In addition, many of you grew up in homes where your father strived to succeed in the workplace while your mother sought to become the perfect homemaker. The husband brought home the bacon, and the wife created the castle for him to come home to. These traditional roles were the norm in modern, urban American society.

As a result, marriage can be like a play in which you and your spouse are cast in the traditional roles of husband (provider) and wife (homekeeper). The roles you play are based on scripts reflecting familial, cultural, and societal attitudes and beliefs about what is normal and appropriate for each gender.

In the new reality of the dual-earner society, however, these traditional roles are often a stumbling block for couples who want to work out new models for mutually shared work and family responsibilities. The traditional, complementary roles you were scripted for and observed in your parents' marriage may live on in your mind and cause problems for your dual-earner marriage. Unless you can identify your particular roles, how you have adjusted to them, and how they work or don't work in your marriage, your relationship may continue to be plagued with conflict, stress, and overload.

Accepting a Role-Sharing Model for Marriage

In a traditional marriage, the husband is the provider and the wife is the homekeeper. The dual-earner marriage, by its very nature, breaks with these traditional roles. By definition, partners in a dual-earner marriage share the provider role. While some couples consider this new reality ideal, others view it as an undesirable reality that must be tolerated.

A major source of potential conflict in the dual-earner marriage can result from the differing degrees to which dual-earner spouses accept the roles in which they find themselves. For wives, the source of conflict may stem from the difference between what you *desire* to be and how you *define* yourself in relationship to the provider and homekeeper roles. For husbands, the conflict usually involves *sharing* the provider and/or homekeeper roles.

Identifying the degree to which you desire to be in a particular role (ideal) and the degree to which you define yourself in that role (real) can help you see how your roles can be a source of stress or satisfaction in your relationship. If there is a great difference between your ideal definition of your role and the reality of your situation, you will experience more dissatisfaction and conflict as a couple. On the other hand, if your ideal definition of your role and the reality of your situation are congruent, you and your spouse will experience more satisfaction and less conflict in your marriage.

Here is a simple way for you and your spouse to reflect on your situation and begin to develop roles that support rather than continue to tax your dual-earner marriage. Answer the following statements with either: 1 = strongly agree, 2 = agree, 3 = disagree, or 4 = strongly disagree.

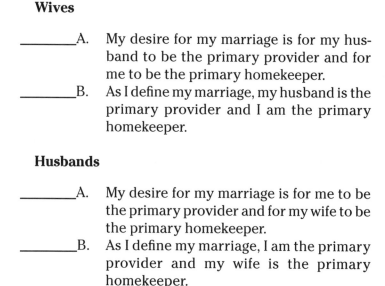

Wives

_____A.   My desire for my marriage is for my husband to be the primary provider and for me to be the primary homekeeper.

_____B.   As I define my marriage, my husband is the primary provider and I am the primary homekeeper.

Husbands

_____A.   My desire for my marriage is for me to be the primary provider and for my wife to be the primary homekeeper.

_____B.   As I define my marriage, I am the primary provider and my wife is the primary homekeeper.

Next, locate your response to each of these statements on the grid for wife or husband on the following page.[1]

For example, in the grid for the wife, the vertical axis reflects her ideal role for herself in her marriage, and the horizontal axis reflects the real, or how she defines her present situation. By locating the combination of your ideal and real responses on the grid, you identify your role category. For example, if you chose *strongly agree* (1) in response to each statement, you are in the *homekeeper/supplemental provider* category. If you responded *strongly disagree* (4) to each statement, you are in the *coprovider/cohomekeeper* category.

Husbands, use the exercise in the same way, plotting your responses on the lower grid. For example, if you chose *strongly agree* (1) in response to each statement, you are in the *provider/uninvolved homekeeper* category. If you responded *strongly disagree* (4) to each statement, you are in the *cohomekeeper/coprovider* category.

It is not important that you fit exactly within one of the categories represented in the grid, but the closer you are to the center, the more able you are to adapt to a number of different situations. When your responses are on the extremes, you show a strong preference for a particular role. If you find yourself in either the lower left or the upper right corner, the conflict between what you perceive to be real and what you desire will have a greater impact on you and on your dual-earner marriage. Conversely, when your desire and your definition coincide (both in upper left or lower right corner), you are more apt to be satisfied with the way things are.

As you read through the following role definitions, notice how each role contributes to or reduces the pressure and strain on the dual-earner marriage. These role descriptions point out the satisfaction level, necessary adjustment, or possible pitfalls likely to accompany each of these dual-earner roles. The descriptions can provide you with clues to why there is conflict in your marriage and how you respond to the tensions created by your dual-earner marriage.

Wife

Ideal				
	strongly agree	1	Homekeeper/ Supplemental Provider	Reluctant Provider
My desire for my marriage is for my husband to be the primary provider and for me to be the primary homekeeper.	agree	2		
	disagree	3	Reluctant Homekeeper	Coprovider/ Cohomekeeper
	strongly disagree	4		

1	2	3	4
strongly agree	agree	disagree	strongly disagree

Real — As I define my marriage, my husband is the primary provider and I am the primary homekeeper.

Husband

Ideal				
	strongly agree	1	Provider/ Uninvolved Homekeeper	Reluctant Homekeeper
My desire for my marriage is for me to be the primary provider and for my wife to be the primary homekeeper.	agree	2		
	disagree	3	Reluctant Provider	Cohomekeeper/ Coprovider
	strongly disagree	4		

1	2	3	4
strongly agree	agree	disagree	strongly disagree

Real — As I define my marriage, I am the primary provider and my wife is the primary homekeeper.

Role Definitions for Wife

Homekeeper/Supplemental Provider

Although a supplemental provider works outside the home, she doesn't view work as a primary area of satisfaction. If you are an employed homekeeper, you earn money to help out with family expenses and to provide some of the extras the family may desire. Even if you are employed full-time, you believe your husband's job is more important, and you see him as the primary provider.

Your loyalty is to your family, not your job; you would rather expend your energies on family, not work. You may feel especially guilty when you can't be available to your children and husband because of your work schedule. If your employer asks you to work overtime, you may resent it because it interferes with your family commitments.

As a group, supplemental providers earn less money than their husbands. As a result, you may wonder if working is worth the time and energy it takes. The more pressured you feel at your job, the more conflict you experience about your role.

Reluctant Homekeeper

Wives who are reluctant homekeepers do not consider employment to be simply a means of making money—they envision a world in which they are equally responsible with their husbands to provide for the family. If you are a reluctant homekeeper, you are not satisfied with your identity as a homekeeper. You desire to be a full participant in the provider role and are frustrated that the reality is otherwise. In her study of homekeepers, Jean Potuchek found that most reluctant homekeepers earn much less than their husbands. She also found that more than 60 percent of them worked part-time, and four out of ten worked twenty-five hours a week or less.[2]

Although you may accept the necessity that your spouse is the primary provider at any one particular point in time, you believe gender should not be the deciding criteria. As a reluctant homekeeper, you are not satisfied with your identity as *just* a homekeeper.

Reluctant Provider

Wives who define themselves in this role see themselves as providing for the basic financial needs of their family but wish they didn't have to work. If you are a reluctant provider, your ideal world is one in which your husband is the sole provider and you are the homekeeper. You have a job in order to pick up the slack after your husband's paycheck is spent. You may earn as much or more than your husband, but you feel stuck in a situation you can't change and that doesn't match your desires. You recognize you can't do it all, but it's difficult to let your spouse get too involved in housework or childcare, since that does not match your ideal for marital roles. You are defined by the world as a coprovider, but in your heart you desire to be a homekeeper. It's difficult for you to accept your plight in life, realizing that much of what you want to do is not possible.

Coprovider/Cohomekeeper

Wives who define themselves as coproviders/cohomekeepers want to work because they enjoy being employed and making money. If you defined yourself as a coprovider, you have gifts and talents that you want to cultivate and develop in the workplace, and it gives you personal satisfaction to extend yourself and expand your potential through your employment. Your contribution to the household is important, and you don't expect your husband to be the sole provider. It does not matter who makes the most money, because the value of your work has to do with the intrinsic satisfaction it brings.

You and your husband both make adjustments in your employment goals when children come along. You find mutually satisfying solutions that take into account personal preference rather than conforming to traditional gender roles. You'll both be involved with your children and adjust your employment responsibilities accordingly. It may be that you'll each cut back to part-time work, or one of you will work part-time for a few years and the other will take a turn later on in the family life cycle. You're invested in your family life as well as in your employment, and you both work to share home responsibilities.

Role Definitions for Husband

Provider/Uninvolved Homekeeper

Some dual-earner husbands have no desire to be involved in homekeeping. They most likely feel threatened having a wife who works. Although husbands in this situation may not wish to admit it, they believe that, while a wife may work outside the home, her primary responsibility is the homekeeping role. Husbands in this role unwittingly force their wives to work at two jobs, one outside the home and the other inside the home. Husbands who are satisfied with this arrangement are likely to discount the economic contribution made by their wife to the marriage. These husbands justify not helping out in the home by deceiving themselves into thinking they are the sole breadwinners and their wife is merely a supplemental provider. These dual-earner husbands can be considered the least well adjusted to their dual-earner status.

Reluctant Provider

Husbands who are reluctant providers do not consider homekeeping to be simply a means of helping out in the home; they envision a world in which they are equally responsible with their wives to care for the home and children. If you are a reluctant provider, you are not satisfied with your identity as a provider. You desire to be a full participant in the homekeeping role and are frustrated that the reality is otherwise. You recognize that wives often earn much less than their husbands and that husbands and wives who desire a more equitable home arrangement often have little support from the workplace, the church, or even friends. Although you may accept the necessity that your wife is the primary homekeeper at any one particular point in time, you want both of you to have the advantages of shared work and family life.

Reluctant Homekeeper

Husbands who have come to define themselves as cohomekeepers but still desire their wife to be the sole homekeeper fit into this category. If you defined yourself this way in the grid, your ideal world is one in which you are the sole provider and your wife is the sole homekeeper. You are sensitive to the reality that, since your wife shares the provider role with you, you need to share the homekeeper role with her. However, your ego may be bruised because this reality is not what you desire, and it may not fit your image of what a man's role should be.

Cohomekeeper/Coprovider

Husbands who are cohomekeepers and coproviders are comfortable with the shared provider/homekeeper role and assume equal responsibility for earning and for homekeeping and childcare. If you both define yourself as a cohomekeeper/coprovider and desire to be one, you recognize the value of maintaining a home and want to participate actively and consistently in raising your children. You have parenting skills and emotional capabilities you want to cultivate and develop in relationship to your children. Your contribution to the home and family is important, and you don't expect your wife to take more than an equal share of the responsibility. You most likely do not experience an identity crisis because your sense of manhood is determined by both work and home values. You have made a positive adjustment to the reality of being part of a dual-earner marriage.

Looking at the Results

Take time now with your spouse to go back and compare your responses to the grid. Do your desires and definitions coincide with or conflict with your spouse's? For example, if your responses fall in corresponding quadrants (e.g., a wife defines herself as a coprovider/cohomekeeper, and a husband defines himself as a cohomekeeper/coprovider), you are likely to experience little conflict related to your dual-earner roles and be better able to mutually empower each other. If, on the other hand, you find that your and your spouse's responses fall in different quadrants (e.g., the wife defines herself as a coprovider/cohomekeeper, and the husband defines himself as a provider/uninvolved homekeeper), your roles may not support each other. The result can be frustration, resentment, conflict, and stress in your marriage.

Winning Combinations

Wife Coprovider/Husband Cohomekeeper

If the wife and husband both fall into the coprovider/cohomekeeper category, your marriage may experience little conflict over roles and responsibilities. You probably aren't concerned about who makes the most money, because you both value your work inside and outside the home for the intrinsic satisfaction it brings. You and your spouse both adjust your employment goals when you have children. You find mutually satisfying solutions that take into account personal preference rather than traditional gender roles. Ideally, you are both involved with your children and can adjust your employment responsibilities accordingly. It may be that you'll each cut back to part-time work, or one will work part-time for a few years and the other will take a turn later on in the family's life cycle. You're both invested equally in your family life and employment and are willing to share responsibilities.

Nina fell into conversation easily when her new boss, Laurel, greeted her warmly at the restaurant where they met to celebrate Nina's first day at her new job as a television marketing representative. This was a welcome change from her stint as a part-time secretary at a local manufacturer. While working part-time, Nina was able to care for her small children—but now things had changed. The kids were both in school full-time, and Nina, always confident she could do it (whatever *it* might be), had taken the plunge.

When Laurel asked how Nina's husband, Charles, felt about her new position, Nina replied, "I think it exhilarates him." Noting the look of skepticism on Laurel's face, Nina continued, "He's been the main breadwinner until now, but we have discussed over the past few years how much I wanted to explore my abilities and test myself. He loves being with the children, and so we finally decided it was time for me to increase my work role outside the home. He'll take more responsibility for the children—picking them up, dropping them off, and helping with homework. I wanted to do an equal share of providing—to come alongside and be an equal partner in the provider and homekeeping roles."

In this case, it was a welcome relief for Charles to have Nina share in the provider role. It gave him freedom to enjoy time with his children as well as take pride in his wife's accomplishments.

Wife Supplemental Provider/Husband Provider

If the wife is a homekeeper/supplemental provider and the husband is a provider/uninvolved homekeeper, you'll probably have a relaxed attitude about your roles. Wives may take on work that is less demanding than a full-time job or a career. Neither of you is pressured—wives to provide or husbands to work in the home. You both assume a middle ground that fits both your values.

Reggie pulled into the driveway, tired from a long day on the floor of the auto showroom. Olivia drove up shortly after, with three-year-old Keenan in tow, having retrieved him from childcare after a full day at her job as bookkeeper at a local pharmacy. Their neighbors and close friends, Harold and Bernice, looked on in pity.

"How do you do it?" Harold yelled across the fence.

"Reggie makes the lion's share and I the lamb's," Olivia answered. "Today I had to leave before my boss was ready for me to go. They know my family comes first."

Olivia and Reggie felt it was appropriate for the husband to be the primary provider, and since Reggie made a larger income and his career was more important to him than Olivia's was to her, it was fine. Olivia wanted to keep busy and make a financial contribution that could help with emergencies and extras. It was important to her to be instrumental in the spiritual life of the family, to encourage Reggie, and teach the children. Reggie supported Olivia's primary role of raising the children and was comfortable working to advance his career to bring in more income to meet the family's future needs.

The one thing that might keep this combination from being a win-win combination is the reality that the marriage is in fact dual-earner. If Reggie and Olivia continue to view their marriage as traditional, they run the risk of denying Olivia's dual roles. Her overcommitment may eventually catch up with her, and their marriage may experience the conflict and stress that result from her overload.

Stress-Producing Combinations

Wife Reluctant Provider/Husband Reluctant Homekeeper

Prior to Dan and Claire's marriage, Claire was a practicing nurse. She saved her money for her hope chest, and soon she and Dan married. Claire got pregnant and had a baby the first year of their marriage. This was her dream come true, and she loved every minute of making a home for her husband and baby. Dan was happy with his job and felt proud to support his new family. This perfect arrangement lasted fifteen years, through the birth of three more children.

In the years that followed, Claire and Dan encountered unexpected additional expenses when they decided to put their children in private schools. Claire reluctantly went back to work as a nurse in a nearby hospital. She soon began to realize how hard it was on her emotionally when she was unable to attend her children's school programs because of her work schedule or when she had to ask other mothers to transport her children to and from extracurricular activities.

Claire and Dan found themselves arguing over who would stay home with a sick child, who would arrange for a babysitter, who would pick up the kids after music lessons, and a host of other details. There seemed to be no way out. Claire was reluctant to be a coprovider but felt she really didn't have a choice. Dan considered himself a provider first and didn't have the flexibility at work to relieve the pressure on Claire. Claire felt she was losing her connection with her family, and Claire and Dan both felt they were losing their connection with each other.

Your marriage may experience stress and tension over roles and responsibilities such as these. Your money concerns seem to compel you into roles neither of you desire for yourselves. The things you value most—for wives, your work in the home, and for husbands, your ability to provide—seem to be out of your reach. You may experience tension, conflict, and a growing lack of intimacy in your marriage. If this is your situation, it is doubly important that you use the conflict resolution skills and the foundation principles in order to work together to ease the pressure and stress and help each other adapt to the roles you find yourselves in.

Wife Reluctant Homekeeper/Husband Reluctant Provider

If you and your spouse are reluctant traditionalists, you may find yourselves struggling because you're both in a situation you don't like. You may be resigned because this is the reality of your life, but neither of you is happy about it. If your family or church promotes a traditional view, you may lack the support to help you create new roles or develop new beliefs. Your irritations may be expressed in blaming or put-downs. In this situation, everyone suffers—the children, the couple, and even their work. Often couples in this situation find that a therapist sensitive to contemporary family issues or a new set of friends can bring a fresh perspective and help them out of their dilemma.

Although these examples illustrating stress-producing combinations are based on couples located in the same quadrants of the grid, there are a number of other stress-producing combinations that occur when a husband and a wife are types in different quadrants. Wives who are coproviders/cohomekeepers will experience different kinds of stress when married to a provider/uninvolved homekeeper, a reluctant homekeeper, or a reluctant provider. Likewise, husbands who are cohomekeepers/coproviders will experience different kinds of stress when married to a homekeeper/supplemental provider, a reluctant provider, or a reluctant homekeeper.

All couples can expect some struggle when defining and adjusting roles in a dual-earner marriage, but when you and your spouse are satisfied with your respective roles and can support each other's desires, you can work together to reduce the conflict and stress in your marriage. Mutual empowerment allows you to take on whatever role satisfies your values and desires.

Supporting Your Spouse's Desire and Definition

The following exercises are designed to help you pinpoint the reasons for some of the tensions you might be experiencing in your dual-earner marriage. They will guide you step-by-step to make the needed changes to clarify your roles and improve your relationship.

> *Week 1.* Each spouse use the grid to identify your preferred provider/homekeeper role. Spend some time thinking about the other options in the figure and how your life would be different if you chose one of them. Make a list of reasons why you prefer your choice. How do you believe your role affects your life and your marriage? Write down the pros and cons of how your role preference affects your personal happiness and the happiness of your marriage.
>
> *Week 2.* Plan a time (approximately forty minutes) in which you agree to come together as husband and wife to compare your role choices. Each spouse take fifteen minutes to explain why you have chosen your provider/homekeeper role and who influenced your beliefs and preferences. The spouse who listens should not be defensive in any way but simply attempt to understand what the preference means to your partner. Make this a safe time of mutual sharing, without conflict. After each spouse has had a turn, take five minutes each to express one thing you especially appreciate about what your spouse has shared.
>
> *Week 3.* Schedule an hour together to compare your role preferences. Identify some of the issues you're dealing with in your dual-earner marriage. Using the list you each prepared during week 1, each spouse

take fifteen minutes to express your thoughts and feelings about your personal happiness and your happiness as a couple. During the last part of this hour, work together to make a list of the difficulties you encounter in your particular dual-earner marriage.

Week 4. Come with emotional openness and creative thoughtfulness about solutions that will make your dual-earner marriage more satisfying. Review the conflict styles in chapter 5 so you can identify your own style and acknowledge your partner's conflict style. Make use of the guidelines for dealing with conflicts that emerge. Take your list from week 3 and each take ten minutes to write down as many solutions as you believe would be mutually agreeable. Share your solutions with each other and pick one from each spouse's list that you will agree to implement the following week. Covenant with each other (it may be helpful to sign a contract) to do your part in following through on that particular solution to make a difference in your married life.

Week 5. Meet for fifteen minutes to review your agreed-upon solution. What are the reasons it's working or not working? What can you do to make necessary adjustments so your solutions will be effective? Keep working and reworking your solutions. You may want to continue meeting each week for fifteen minutes to discuss your progress. Remember, you can come up with new solutions any time. Doing the unexpected or coming up with fresh ideas tends to keep the marriage vital.

You will find that the ability to work together to create a satisfactory division of work, family, and home responsibilities may be more important than which roles you choose. When there is a mutual perception of fairness, appreciation, and unity, conflicts decrease, stress is reduced, and both partners can be empowered to do what gives you the most happiness personally and as a couple.

7

An Extra Dose
of Adaptability

Marshall and Penny decided that theirs would be a marriage unlike either of their parents'. Marshall had grown up in affluence: His father was the only banker of their medium-size town in Tennessee. His work consumed him to the point that he was more of a banker than a father. His mother's life was high society. She rarely involved herself in day-to-day household chores, thanks to their maid and cook. Marshall was virtually raised by the nanny.

Marshall followed his father and became a banker in the Chicago area. There he met Penny, the daughter of a single-parent home from a middle-class family in St. Louis. Penny's mother had always worked outside of the home, so Penny had little time with her mother and rarely saw her father. After Penny and Marshall were married, she established herself as a successful real estate broker.

All seemed well for the first three years, until Penny and Marshall had their first child. Gretchen's birth gave rise to the old issues of absentee parenting for both Marshall and Penny. In the initial years they both made gallant efforts to be with Gretchen as much as possible. But soon, Marshall began spending more time at work, ostensibly to get ahead in a competitive economy. Penny, too, began to work more hours to make a better life for their daughter. Not until they started talking about hiring a nanny for Gretchen did they realize what was happening. When they took a good look at themselves and saw they were following in the footsteps of their parents, they did a deliberate about-face and reestablished parenting as a priority in their lives.

Both of them made a deliberate choice to cut back hours at work in order to give home life their highest priority. They agreed that emotional connections and relationships are far more important than material things. They also discovered that their faith provided a set of values that helped them revamp their lives.

Marriage is like being on a stage playing respective husband and wife roles that have been scripted by cultural and societal attitudes and beliefs. It can become a baffling task for a dual-earner couple to find a script that fits their particular circumstance. The traditional homemaker and single wage-earner roles are stifling and unrealistic for many couples today. As a result, the dual-earner couple must create and adjust to new roles to satisfy their unique values and life situation, but this can sometimes be harder than you think. If you vary too much from the original script, you might get booed off the stage. On the other hand, if you follow the traditional script too closely, you undermine your chances to adjust to new roles and successfully combine your work and family life.

Dual-earner couples face unique challenges when adjusting to new marital, work, and family roles. A wife may feel guilt for breaking old, prescriptive norms, or she may experience depression if her husband feels threatened by her coprovider status or questions the benefit of the dual-earner marriage altogether.

For Wives Only

Even though there have been valiant attempts to decrease gender-specific messages in children's books, and even though women are increasingly visible in the workplace and in high public offices, society continues to glorify the image of mothering and homemaking. Is it any wonder, then, that women who are dual-earners are hit with the dreaded "guilty wives syndrome"? Brought up to believe women should be responsible for caretaking and homemaking, you may feel extreme guilt if your time and energy is split between work and home life. As a result, women who work outside of the home spend significantly more time than their husbands caring for their children and for the home.

Guilty Wives Syndrome

In her study of working women, Arlie Hochschild cites two reasons why women who work outside of the home still do more of the housework and take on more responsibility for childcare:[3]

1. Women who earn *less* than their husbands do more housework and childcare because they feel guilty and want to equalize their contribution to the marriage.
2. Women who earn *more* than their husbands also do more housework in order to relieve the guilt they feel about earning a higher wage.

In this no-win situation, it is no wonder wives in dual-earner marriages feel guilty!

Marianne realized that things had gone too far the day she came home from work and had an ugly encounter with her teenage daughter. Marianne was a college professor and was able to arrange her schedule so she could be available to her children and help with their extracurricular activities. After hours, she also kept a spotless house, entertained frequently in her home, and served as a volunteer in her church. One day when she was particularly exhausted, she balked at the idea of driving her daughter and friends to cheerleading practice. When she suggested that another mother drive for a change, her daughter turned, looked her in the eye, and exclaimed, "Their mothers work!" Marianne was shocked at her daughter's lack of appreciation for the fact that she, too, had a full-time job outside the home. The guilty wives syndrome had given the false impression that she could do it all and contributed to a distorted picture of who she was.

Close to burnout from the effects of the guilty wives syndrome, Marianne made a turnabout then and there. She announced to her husband and children that she had been living a charade and change was long overdue. Her family had not realized what a toll this superwoman role had taken on Marianne. The guilty wives syndrome had kept her on overload for six years.

Just the Facts, Ma'am

Even though by definition, partners in a dual-earner marriage share the breadwinner role, it may not be the case that husbands in these marriages share equally in the homekeeper role. As a result, women who work outside of the home still do more of the housework and take on more responsibility for childcare.

In her book, *The Second Shift*, Arlie Hochschild labels the after-hours family work that must be done when two spouses return home from a busy work day as the "second shift." When partners spend a great deal of time and energy in their respective jobs, they return home tired and depleted, and though neither is emotionally or physically equipped to manage the second shift, someone has to do it. It's usually the woman who takes on the major portion of this work. In fact, when Hochschild calculated the additional work performed by the average dual-earner wife, she discovered it amounted to an extra month of twenty-four-hour days each year.[4] No wonder women experience overload! You are working not one, but two full-time jobs.

Why is it the wife who takes on the majority of the second-shift work? Hochschild's study can help us understand the answer to this question. When asked, both husbands and wives agreed that housework should be shared, but the truth of the matter is *husbands think they help out more than they do.*

Husbands in dual-earner marriages do help out more in the home than sole-provider husbands, but they spend an average of only twenty minutes per day. In addition, when these husbands do work in the home, they are selective about the tasks they are willing to do. Few men assume responsibility for washing dirty clothes, cleaning toilets, scrubbing floors, or a host of other unpleasant tasks. They agree to help out with shopping and caring for the children, but even when they do take care of the children, they spend time playing with them rather than getting them dressed for school or taking care of them when they're sick.

In addition, both husbands *and* wives believed the second shift was the *wife's* responsibility. So even when husbands share household chores, the wives take on the responsibility of managing and organizing the tasks.

Why Do I Feel Depressed?

A husband's lack of support for his wife's employment has consistently been found to be a significant source of tension in marriage. When there is incongruence between your husband's beliefs about what is right (ideal) and your experience of what is (real), you will experience a significant impact on the degree of satisfaction or dissatisfaction in your marriage.

Your husband's attitudes about work roles, marriage roles, and personal roles determine his reactions to your dual-earner status. His reactions, if critical or unfavorable, can greatly impact your emotional well-being.

If your husband's ideal is the traditional *complementary* model of marriage roles and you work full-time, it can disrupt his ideal image of himself as sole breadwinner and provider. If his perception of what it means to be an adequate man is to be the sole provider, your dual-earner status may threaten his sense of masculinity. Even though he may agree that you need to work to help pay the bills, your dual-earner status can become a source of tension because it's inconsistent with how he thinks things *should* be. This places you in a difficult position because your employment serves to define him as a failure in his own eyes.

Studies have consistently found that a husband's discontent with and lack of support for his wife's dual-earner status is a significant source of tension in marriage. Patricia Ulbrich's study of 682 dual-earner couples linked husbands' lack of support with depression among dual-earner wives. Wives commonly complained of depression when their husbands were either opposed to or had a negative attitude about their employment.[5]

Curt and Becky had a rocky time financially when they moved from a small town to a big city. Although the move meant a good promotion for Curt, the standard of living and housing expenses in the city meant that Becky had to go to work. She was glad to contribute to the family and was excited about bringing home her paycheck each week, but she faced Curt's disapproval. It was not long before she began depositing her earnings in the bank without mentioning it to Curt.

Curt neither acknowledged Becky's financial contribution nor showed appreciation for her part in supporting the family. As their relationship grew increasingly more distant, Becky became more sullen and discouraged. She enjoyed her work and the people there, and she felt proud of her earning power. It seemed Curt was asking her to give up an important part of herself so he could feel good about himself. This not only dampened her spirits, but it also decreased her respect for him. Since she did not consider divorce an option, she remained in the marriage with a constant, low-grade depression.

While some husbands appreciate their wife's financial contribution, others not only fail to appreciate but actually devalue their wife's dual-earner status. The hours she puts in at work either produce no response or a negative response. If, on the other hand, the wife has no interest in being employed and works grudgingly, she is apt to minimize herself and her efforts. The discrepancy she feels between the ideal and the real causes stress. When women get caught between a traditional complementary marriage ideal and the necessity of earning money to make ends meet, the stress may also lead to depression.

Tom and Susan began their marriage with similar ideals and beliefs about the husband being the sole breadwinner, but when they found themselves in financial straights, Susan went to work. Tom admits he was threatened when Susan brought home her first paycheck.

He feared she would have less respect for him, and that his power would diminish. His fears were allayed as they intentionally dialogued about how to manage their dual-earner home. They agreed that Susan would have more say in how the money was spent, but they would make decisions jointly as a sign of their commitment to each other and the family.

Their mutual desire to make decisions that would benefit their marriage and family helped them redefine their previous notions of power. Tom realized that a cooperative role-sharing model meant he no longer carried the entire burden of providing for the family. In addition, since Susan liked details, she took over the budgeting and bookkeeping, while Tom exercised his visionary nature by making financial investments. This allowed them to trust, respect, and appreciate each other in ways that mutually empowered them. Their mutual acceptance of Susan's new dual-earner status enhanced rather than disrupted their marriage and provided new avenues of self-expression and self-esteem for both of them.

For Husbands Only

Not all husbands are alike in their ability to handle a dual-earner marriage and the role sharing that it requires. When you charted your role definition and desire, you were able to identify the degree to which you desire to be and to which you define yourself in a homekeeper role. How comfortable were you with the role? Were you a cohomekeeper, a reluctant provider, a reluctant homekeeper, or a provider/uninvolved homekeeper? Your preference for one role or another is, in part, conditioned by how you define your male self-image.

Inadequate Husband Syndrome

Since, by definition, partners in a dual-earner marriage share the provider role, husbands who think it is their duty to be the sole provider may feel inadequate when their wife makes a contribution to the family's finances or when they feel that what they earn is not enough. Such husbands may not be opposed to their wife's working outside of the home for the sake of personal fulfillment—they may even be proud of their wife if her work is a creative outlet or of service to others. But when her work is defined as an economic necessity, a husband may feel that his masculinity is threatened, and he may feel inadequate as a result.

For the first fifteen years of their marriage, Roger was the wage earner and Candace took care of the home and the day-to-day care of their three children. As the children approached their teen years, Roger and Candace realized that Roger's salary would not be enough to make ends meet. They had made an increasing number of major purchases on credit in the last two years, and now the monthly bills were nearly equal to Roger's monthly income. Roger and Candace agreed that Candace would return to teaching, her profession before they married. While this solved the economic problem, it created another: Roger felt inadequate because he alone could not earn enough money to meet his family's needs. He experienced what many husbands experience when their wife has to work—the inadequate husband syndrome.

At the core of the inadequate husband syndrome is a lack of self-worth. When you continue to define your worth based on the traditional role stereotypes, tying your identity solely to the provider role, your self-worth is fragile. Men who suffer from the inadequate husband syndrome are in need of liberation from a narrow and outmoded definition of manhood.

Dual-Earner Husbands and Housework

There is evidence that some men refrain from greater participation in housework out of fear for what it would do to their self-image. One study found that husbands who were aggressive, dominant, and emotionally tough helped out less than men who were expressive toward their wives.[6] The emotionally tough men were more comfortable assuming the traditional male tasks of mowing the lawn, taking care of the car, and making minor household repairs.

Not surprisingly, husbands who were more flexible in their self-definition also believed in egalitarian roles. They assumed more responsibility for housework than husbands who held rigid, traditional attitudes about their manhood.

When you are a truly liberated man, you will see beyond the stereotypes. You will not only accept your wife as a coprovider, but you will be secure enough in your manhood to wash a dish or change a diaper.

Costs and Benefits

Ask a man from a dual-earner marriage whether it's worth it to give up the stereotypes and have his wife employed, and his mind is likely to begin calculating the costs versus the benefits. The bottom line for most dual-earner husbands is that if the benefits outweigh the costs, then you say it's worth it. If the costs are greater than the benefits, then you say it is not.

What do you consider to be the costs and benefits of your dual-earner marriage? You might find your responses reflected in a study of fifty-seven men, comparing the costs and benefits of their dual-earner marriage.[7] (See next page.)

While you may be accustomed to seeing only the costs to your identity and comfort, your greater involvement in the home can have some unexpected benefits as well. When you are the sole provider in your family, your job greatly reduces the time you can spend with your children. When you share the provider role, you spend more time with your children and have more opportunities to get involved in their activities and to know them as people. As you become more involved with your children, you will become a more complete person socially and emotionally. You can learn to expand your emotional expressiveness from such things as bringing home gifts, taking the family out for milkshakes, reading a short bedtime story to the kids, or being able to listen to and consider your children's personal and emotional issues. You will be able to develop valuable interpersonal skills such as empathy and genuine responsiveness.

In contrast to the world of work, where you are expected to make decisions based on the rational rather than the emotional, taking care of your children inclines you to consider personal and emotional issues. This will not only benefit you in your home life, but it can have a positive impact on your work life as well. By developing your empathy skills, you will become more effective in relating to the people you work with daily. Organizational management theory now stresses that personnel in the business world must understand the social and emotional needs of workers. Increased involvement with your children will help you develop skills that can complement the traditional male tendencies toward rationality and emotional control.

When you share the provider role, your family does not depend entirely on your income. This gives you

Costs and Benefits
of the Dual-Earner Marriage

Costs	Men Reporting
Stress due to physical and emotional overload	71%
Decrease in leisure time	51%
Increased time spent on household tasks	47%
Decreased sexual activity due to exhaustion or lack of time	41%
Decreased opportunities for career placement	32%
Multiple role demands	25%
Less time for emotional life with wife	25%

Benefits	Men Reporting
Increased income	98%
Greater contentment of wife	96%
Wife's independent identity	88%
Wife's greater opportunity for social interaction	82%
Less pressure to provide economically	71%
Greater rewards from parenting	58%

Source: Adapted from L. Gilbert, *Men in Dual-Career Families: Current Realities and Future Prospects* (Hillsdale, N.J.: Erlbaum, 1985).

more flexibility to make decisions that affect your family's welfare.

Roland had been working for a large corporation for the past twelve years. During that time, he had been asked three times to move his family to a new city in order to take advantage of opportunities for promotion. Because his wife was settled at her job, he had declined the offers. When he learned that he was in line for a top managerial position more than a thousand miles away from his family's home, he knew he could consider other options. His wife, Jill, loved their home and neighborhood. Lisa, a sophomore in high school, and eleven-year-old Mike wouldn't want to leave their friends. Since Jill was a coprovider, the family was free to consider the opportunity without pressure to accept the transfer and promotion.

Perhaps the greatest benefit of a dual-earner marriage is that it facilitates your liberation as a male in a unique way. When you are a coprovider and cohomekeeper, you have the opportunity to regard your spouse as a peer and your children and home as your coresponsibility. From this perspective, you can embrace a rich and varied life, full of opportunities to learn more about your feelings, express more of your attitudes, and come to understand where many of those feelings and attitudes originated. You have a unique opportunity for self-discovery. This opens the door to a new freedom to choose new methods and approaches rather than relying on the old behaviors that were a result of upbringing and enculturation.

A dual-earner marriage provides the opportunity for increased intimacy with spouse and children. There is so much to give and receive from each other's varied experiences and perspectives, and all of it will contribute to your ability to grow with the ever-changing circumstances in the workplace, the home, the marriage, and with each other.

For Couples Still Struggling with Shared Home Involvement

As a husband, you may still be struggling in your dual-earner marriage with the issues of equitable sharing of housework and childcare. As a wife, you may still struggle with feelings of guilt or depression. We suggest that you and your spouse engage in a brief experiment. For one week, as completely as possible, give *all* of the second-shift duties to one spouse. The free spouse is allowed to help out only when it is absolutely impossible for the responsible spouse to do the work. Then for one week exchange roles so that the free spouse takes over all of the second-shift duties.

Once you have completed this experiment, take the weekend off. Hire someone to take care of the children, if you have children, and head for your favorite getaway. Share with each other your experiences during the two one-week periods. After you both feel assured that the other has a complete understanding of the many responsibilities involved in the second shift, negotiate a mutually empowering sharing of responsibilities for the second-shift tasks. You may be surprised to find how quickly you can relieve overload, increase the satisfaction between you as a couple, and enhance your lives as a couple and individually by providing new avenues for self-expression and self-esteem.

In our current dual-earner society, traditional, idealized roles are often a stumbling block to couples who want to work out a new model of mutually shared work and family responsibilities. You may struggle with guilt, depression, or lack of self-worth, or you may even question your identities in the process. But it is worth the effort. The truth is, couples who fail to work out shared responsibility for household duties will continue to experience stress, overload, and marital tension, whereas couples who work out equitable sharing will relieve many of the pressures on the marriage and be more content.

All couples who have worked together to adjust to new roles and to work out mutually shared household responsibilities agree that getting to an equitable arrangement is a difficult but rewarding journey. When you work together in your new roles, you create a deeper sense of connection and commitment, empowering each other to full responsibility within your dual-earner marriage and in your work life.

Stages of Marriage

You Aren't the Person I Thought I Married

When we give a marriage retreat, Jack often begins by saying, "I've been involved in six different marriages in my life. . . . " After allowing the shock to set in—with the participants wondering why he is leading a marriage retreat—he continues by saying, ". . . all to the same woman."

Dual-earner marriages are not static; they are dynamic and ever changing. Sometimes that change is so drastic that the relationship is best thought of as another marriage. Marriage, like individuals and families, can best be understood as developing through predictable life-cycle stages. Within each marital stage, certain key developmental tasks must be accomplished in order for the marriage to successfully progress to the next stage. Likewise, there are developmental tasks that must be performed by each marital partner at each particular stage.

Some developmental tasks are stage-specific; that is, they must be mastered at a specific stage and no other.

Other tasks can begin to be mastered at one stage and will continue to be mastered at all subsequent stages. For example, in the first year of marriage it is necessary for you as a couple to master the task of establishing your own household. In contrast, interpersonal communication is a skill that you will work on throughout the marital life cycle.

As Jack said, we have experienced many different marriages in each stage of our relationship. That is quite normal. It may be helpful, when you and your spouse begin to fear that your marriage has changed beyond recognition, to think about and identify your many marriages, realizing that the process of change is normal. We have detailed four general stages below and described some of the many different marriages that may occur during each stage.

The Marital Dyad

When two people marry, a new relationship begins in the form of a dyad—a committed relationship between two people. The major developmental task at this first stage of marriage involves the husband and wife adjusting to each other in their new roles as married rather than single persons.

There is an incredible agenda to be accomplished by dual-earner couples during this stage. While continuing to hold jobs outside of the home, you must set up a new household, divide the household chores, create a financial budget, make sexual adjustments, develop mutual friendships, plan social events, make decisions about church involvement and spiritual growth, and the list of tasks goes on. Given the difficulty of balancing two jobs with home life, it is extremely important at this stage that you establish a solid foundation for the future.

Besides adjusting to marital roles, each spouse needs to complete the individual developmental task of differentiating from your family of origin. If you continue to be highly emotionally or financially dependent upon your parents, you will be unable to cleave to your spouse because you have failed to leave your parents. If you as a young married couple want to successfully build a firm foundation for your marriage, you need to leave parents and cleave to each other so that you can be united in establishing a new household.

The Honeymoon Marriage

For the two of us, the honeymoon phase of our marriage lasted about three years. As you would expect, there is much romance in this marriage. At this stage, you may try to live up to a fantasy charade, presenting yourselves to others as the perfect couple. You may try hard not to argue or have a disagreement—certainly not admitting it to others if you do. You attempt to be what you think family and friends expect you to be as you learn the new tasks and roles of marriage.

In this marriage you also begin to establish your own traditions. You celebrate birthdays, Christmas, and special holidays, and in the process develop your own unique family rituals. Learning to accept your differences and giving each other the freedom to be unique individuals is the major challenge.

Most couples benefit from having at least two years in the honeymoon marriage to adjust to being married and to have sufficient time to accomplish the tasks required of newlyweds. The early arrival of a child can prematurely shift the focus of attention from the tasks of the marriage dyad to those of the parent/ child relationship.

Married with Young Children

The obvious initiating event of this second marital stage is the birth or adoption of the first child. When your dyad becomes a triad, there are a number of relationship issues that you must work through. Changing the existing marital system to include the new member can be an especially hard adjustment after you have enjoyed the freedom, lack of heavy financial responsibilities, and unencumbered time of the earlier marriage. As a couple you must set new boundaries, provide new space, and find new ways of relating in order to accommodate the new member.

A newborn is totally dependent on the care of others. In the single-earner marriage, one spouse is available to give needed care to the child. However, as a dual-earner couple, you must learn the art of juggling two work schedules around your child's needs. When this can't be done, suitable substitute childcare becomes a major concern. (See chapter 13 for a discussion of alternative childcare options available to dual-earner couples.)

The Madonna and the Provider Marriage

In this marriage, a husband may start his first big job, often at the same time that a wife gives birth to the first child. A second child may arrive shortly after the first. In this marriage, couples find they have highly differentiated or separated roles. The wife, the Madonna (as in mother, not pop singer), devotes most of her waking hours to cooking, cleaning, washing, and caring for small children. The husband, the provider, is busy preparing for business meetings or other work-related events.

During this time couples have made a little progress on allowing each other more freedom to be themselves, but they often continue to live idealized roles. In fact, in some ways, couples can add to the idealization that began in the honeymoon marriage. Wives may try to become the ideal wife and mother, striving to become a gourmet cook, an interior decorator, and a supermother all at the same time. Husbands may eagerly attempt to establish themselves in their professions, seeking advancement and striving to be a loving and considerate husband and devoted father.

The Double Duty Marriage

When both parents work outside the home, married couples with young children are often overwhelmed with the need for a double dose of energy. After a long day at work, they come home and need some quality time with their children, while at the same time they need to take care of many household duties.

An advantage for these couples may be the special appreciation they have for their children after being separated all day. Parents can reap the rewards of spending focused time with their young children during these high-demand years, but to make it happen, something has to go! The wise couple in a double duty marriage will put the priority on their relationship with each other.

The White Picket Fence Marriage

During this marriage, a couple may buy their first home, and frequently the husband is busy working to support his family's growing needs. While husbands work, wives may continue to be the supermother and housewife. The wife may remain economically dependent on her husband, while the husband is emotionally dependent on his wife.

Toward the end of this marriage, a husband may struggle to free himself of his emotional dependence on his wife. A wife may start wondering who she is as a person in her own right. "Is there life beyond children? Am I more than just a wife and mother?" she may ask.

With our move to a university in another region of the country, we bought our first house—a four-bedroom ranch in the suburbs. Jack was busy teaching and attempting to publish so he wouldn't perish. Judy was busy parenting and homekeeping.

Since Judy had worked while Jack finished graduate school, she was more than willing to be "just" a housewife and mother. Jack was unsure if he could survive under the academic pressure of the university, and he needed Judy's reassurance. His shyness also made him dependent on Judy's extrovertedness in social situations. We became mutually dependent on each other in this marriage.

Toward the end of this marriage, the sameness of suburban life—coffee lunches, afternoon soap operas, volunteer work, and the like—became boring for Judy. Was she more than just a professor's wife? For his part, Jack struggled to free himself from his emotional dependence on Judy. This marriage lasted seven years.

The Turbulent Marriage

At any point in the dual-earner marriage there can be unexpected turbulence (e.g., illness, job loss, accident, extended family issues). These life circumstances demand time and energy that put a severe drain on the dual-earner couple. There is not much flexibility in the work world to deal with these disruptions. It may require one spouse to take on an extra load at work while the other takes time away.

This marriage, consisting of much change and shake-up, can occur when a wife decides to go back to work or school to prepare for her own career. This change makes it necessary for a husband to assume many of the housework responsibilities. Conflict over roles and standards is likely to occur. The need for both husbands and wives to balance involvement outside of the home with involvement within the home can cause strain in even the ideal relationship.

When our children were in grammar school, Judy decided to go back to graduate school to prepare for her own career. This made it necessary for Jack to assume many of the housework responsibilities. Conflict began when Judy assessed Jack's housework as not up to her standards. Jack was also given the task of preparing several evening meals each week. Fortunately, those cooking classes he'd taken in high school came in handy.

Up until this marriage, most parenting was done by Judy. When Judy began school, Jack needed to be available each school day at 3 P.M. to take care of our children when they returned home from school. This also began our coparenting, as Jack became more involved in the discipling and nurturing of our children. We found we differed in our views of how the children should be raised, and this upset things in the beginning.

Several years into this marriage, our son, Jeff, was very unexpectedly diagnosed with bone cancer. He died just four months later. With a shake-up in our traditional ways of being a husband and wife, and grieving the loss of our son, we found our "ideal" relationship was under a refining fire. However, our faith in God and our strong foundational covenant commitment brought us to deeper levels of intimacy in the depths of the turmoil and trial.

Married with Teenagers

When children reach adolescence, increased pressure is put on the marital system. Dual-earner marriages need an extra dose of flexibility, and this flexibility will be severely tested by adolescent children. Adolescents want freedom, but if work prevents you from giving your children needed attention and guidance, the combination of greater physical mobility made possible by driving privileges can result in an unhealthy, unmonitored freedom.

Adolescence is a time when children begin to differentiate and separate from their parents. If you have not developed a strong, emotionally bonded relationship with your children, as adolescents they will not have the personal security to begin a healthy differentiation from you.

Adolescents need to exert their independence while establishing a healthy separate identity. If you feel good about yourself, you will be able to accept this and not be threatened by what you see as a passing need in your children. However, children's adolescence often coincides with your approaching midlife, which often involves stress of its own. Stress generated by your job can contribute to a state of midlife crisis if you

> feel that you have become obsolete as a worker.
> develop a fear of being overtaken at work by a younger, bettertrained person.
> realize that you will not reach the lofty goals you set years before.
> lack motivation for work—commonly known as "career burnout."
> realize that you have become a workaholic, unable to relax when away from the job.

When parents and adolescent children are all struggling with their own identity crises at the same time, the result can be increased conflicts. If you are experiencing midlife crisis, you will not be as psychologically prepared to handle rejection from your child. Both you and your children have personal needs that put demands on your relationship. If you are not in crisis, you will be better able to be patient and understanding with your adolescent. It is also true that if your child has already established a clear sense of self and is not in the midst of an identity crisis, he or she will be in a better position to be supportive of you during your time of need.

One of the chief factors in parent/adolescent conflicts may be that the parent in midlife and the adolescent are experiencing opposite physical effects. At a time when the adolescent is just beginning to develop the physical characteristics of adulthood, you may be beginning to lose yours. While the adolescent boy finds his muscles growing and his physical strength increasing, the father finds his muscles shrinking and his strength declining. While the adolescent girl begins to develop a nice figure, her mother is fighting hard to keep her figure intact. The one is just developing increased physical beauty and capabilities; the other is losing them.

The Dual-Earner Marriage

The dual-earner marriage, whether it has been part of the marriage all along or a shift along the way, has both rewards and tensions. It involves the challenge of finding strength in separateness as well as strength in connectedness. We believe this is an ongoing effort at all times for couples. Most of us experience the ups and downs of being close and feeling distant, and it takes conscious effort to maintain a good balance. Whereas it is normal to oscillate between these two points for all couples, there is a tendency for dual-earner couples to gravitate to the "separate and distant" side.

After we survived the turmoil and shake-up of our turbulent marrriage, we entered our dual-career marriage. In this marriage we did more individuation. We learned to be less dependent on each other and to establish our own identities. Judy completed her doctoral degree and no longer thought of herself as a professor's wife but as a marriage and family therapist. She had an identity that gave her a new sense of self-confidence.

In feeling less dependent on each other, we learned to live parts of our lives independent of the other. But we also wondered how to do this and still remain close to each other in new ways. This began a period of challenge as to how to keep the marriage vital and meaningful while enjoying our separate careers.

Just as we began to adapt to being a dual-earner couple, two important things happened. First, our daughter, Jacque, became a teenager, and second, we adopted a ten-year-old Korean son, Joel. Given the changes in our family, we sought family therapy—not because we were doing that bad, but because we could benefit from outside help in processing all the changes that had occurred. This marriage lasted about ten years.

The Empty Nest Marriage

When all the children have left home, parents are supposed to experience the "empty nest syndrome," which is characterized by depression and a struggle to redefine marital roles. However, for most couples this marital stage is experienced as one of freedom and relief that the kids are finally gone! Family psychologist John Rosemond has humorously observed that the empty nest means

> always being able to find a parking space in the driveway.
> picking up the phone to make a call, and the line is free.

not waiting up until the children get home.
not having to listen to their music.
the refrigerator has food in it.[8]

Research confirms that, other than the first years of marriage, spouses report the empty nest years to be the happiest years of their married life. Without children around, dual-earner marriages at this stage tend to be free of overload. One obvious reason for this is that couples have increased amounts of time to be with each other or to do as they choose. In addition, couples experience relief from the financial burden of supporting a household of children. A common exception to this, however, is that parents are expected to pay large amounts of money to educate their college-age children.

A major developmental task of this marital stage is accepting the aloneness created by the children's departure. If children were the couple's major common focus, this can be a period of great disillusionment and loneliness. Such a couple may find that they have very little in common now that the children have left home.

In single-earner homes, the stay-at-home parent (usually the mother) may experience depression when the children leave. The empty nest is, in fact, one major reason a wife will seek employment outside of the home. Working outside of the home can help cushion the impact of the loss of the mothering role.

Given the expanded life expectancy in our society, the empty nest stage accounts for nearly half of the length of the typical marriage. Thus, it is imperative that a married couple actively create the type of work and home situation that will allow them and their relationship to remain physically, psychologically, and socially healthy.

The Dynamic-Duo Marriage

This marriage occurs when both spouses are successfully engaged in careers and have found ways to create a lot of togetherness. At the same time, you have launched your children and are experiencing the pleasures of the empty nest. Most of your concerns do not stem from your marriage relationship, but from the sense of responsibility for your aging parents and children who are emotionally and financially dependent on you.

We have found this marriage to be a productive time for us as a couple. We teach, write, travel, and lead workshops together. At times we get into a dynamic *duel* with so much togetherness, but we find that our history of working through conflicts and developing intimacy is a great resource for those times. We seek to balance our personal needs in a supportive interdependency.

The Later Years

A major developmental task that emerges after the empty nest stage is dealing with the aging process. A couple must learn to accept and make appropriate responses to the physical effects of aging. Retirement also presents a major development task to be mastered by the dual-earner couple.

While both are working, a husband and wife are likely to have their own network of friends cultivated from their years at work. However, retirement cuts them off from this source of social support. The retired dual-earner couple may be surprised at how much their jobs were a part of their lives. In retirement they will need to be together more and will therefore need to coordinate their lives together.

The Bobbsey Twins Marriage

The next marriage, which emerges after retirement, was described by a woman in her sixties this way: "We are the Bobbsey Twins, we do everything together. We get up at the same time, eat our meals together, shop together, watch TV together, socialize together, and go to bed at the same time."

Often wives in this marriage say, "Since my husband retired I don't know what to do with him. He's around all the time." Husbands may comment, "I'm just so glad when she goes off with her friends so I can be alone for a while."

Although there is much good-natured joking between elderly husbands and wives over too much togetherness, there is probably some truth underlying the banter. One of the best things about the retirement years for a dual-earner couple is that they can have quantity time together. But they would also do well to intentionally carve out some time to pursue their own separate interests.

Often the ill health of one or both spouses can dampen an older couple's time together. Some must resign themselves to the role of caretaker for a partner who is in ill health. Aging, both in its physical and psychological forms, is a fact of life that each of us must contend with. If a couple will give thanks for the fact that they have a spouse who is surviving with them, the later marriage years can be a time of much joy and fulfillment.

Naming Your Marriages

Naming your different marriages can be very helpful to couples who are trying to understand the stages of their marriage. It is a relatively simple task, and we suggest that you and your spouse find an hour in which you are free to talk and reminisce about the years you have spent together as husband and wife. Think back to when you were first married. Recall the feelings you had toward each other and about life in general. What was your shared reality—did you view life optimistically, pessimistically, ideally, or realistically? How did you and your spouse define your marriage roles? What were your expectations for each other as a husband and a wife? What tasks were done separately and which were shared? Ask yourselves these and related questions as a means of getting in touch with the way your marriage was in the past.

After discussing your first several years of marriage, ask these same questions about your marriage over time. As you do, be aware of the way in which your answers to these questions change. When you and your spouse detect a significant change in the makeup of your marriage, try to give it a name. Some of your marriages may be very brief, lasting only several years, while others may last a decade.

The names you give to your marriage may be similar to the ones we have suggested (most of us do start with a honeymoon type marriage), but they may also be quite unique. The important thing is that the name symbolizes where you and your spouse were socially, psychologically, physically, and spiritually at each stage in your married life.

By naming your marriages, you have a chance to appreciate the dynamic nature of marriage and also to realize that, in spite of the many changes, you can still remain connected. Your one-flesh union remains constant even though the form of your marriages may vary.

9

The Elaborate Balancing Act

In single-earner families, the marital roles tend to be complementary and are divided according to work in the home and work outside the home. In dual-earner marriages, the marital roles tend to be interdependent and must be divided according to each couple's unique preferences based on their personalities and abilities. Couples must work together—communicating, negotiating, and compromising—to create and adapt to these new roles and shared responsibilities inside the home, even though roles outside the home are well defined.

When couples in a dual-earner marriage begin this process, you may at first feel like you're part of an elaborate balancing act. How do you keep the complicated structure of work and home life from collapsing beneath you? It takes a great amount of agility to balance your new roles and to juggle work and family life! This agility comes from having the right amounts of adaptability, flexibility, and cohesion in your marriage relationship.

When these elements are present in your marriage, you can successfully balance demanding roles inside and outside of the home.

Adaptability: How Adaptable Are You?

As you might surmise, couples who want to relieve the pressure, decrease stress, and grow together in a dual-earner marriage must be adaptable—able to change and share roles as circumstances demand. How able are you as a couple to adapt to the different roles required in your dual-earner marriage?

A range for a couple's adaptability in marital roles is shown below. The far left side of the continuum represents a couple who rigidly adheres to prescribed roles and is determined to play them out according to a pre-determined script. This couple never varies from the script, even when circumstances call for an adjustment. The far right side represents the couple who plays out vaguely defined roles that are so loosely ordered that their life is chaotic. The middle categories identify couples who accept moderately structured roles but adapt when necessary and as circumstances require.

Degree of Adaptability in Marital Role

low ····· 1 ···· 2 ····· 3 ···· 4 ····· 5 ···· 6 ····· 7 ···· 8 ···· 9 ·····10····· high

          Rigid   Structured   Flexible   Chaotic

Take a moment to rate your marriage on the adaptability scale. Below are five statements for you and your spouse to answer separately. Read each of the following statements and then rate your marriage in terms of marital adaptability on a scale from one (rigid) to ten (chaotic) for each statement.

1. We are flexible in how we handle differences.
2. We shift household responsibilities between us.
3. We freely say what we want.
4. We try new ways of dealing with problems.
5. When problems arise, we compromise.

After you have completed scoring all five statements, simply add up the five scores. The scores will fall between a potential low of five (rigid) and high of fifty (chaotic); the midpoint represents a flexibly structured, or highly adaptable relationship. Scores below twenty-five indicate your marriage falls in the more structured range, while scores above twenty-five indicate your marriage is in the more flexible range. Now compare your scores with each other.

If your total score is at the lower end of the scale (both spouses have similar low scores), you tend to adhere to rigid roles and may not be able to adapt to the changing roles demanded by the dual-earner reality. You may experience frustration that life doesn't conform to your ideal, and you may refuse to give an inch to meet your spouse halfway in sharing responsibilities. In this case, you will want to cultivate adaptability in your marriage.

If your total score is higher than forty, you may be in a runaway situation. Extreme adaptability leads to chaotic or out-of-control feelings and behavior. This should be a red flag for the marriage. You'll need to find ways to structure your roles to put more predictability and less stress-producing chaos into your life.

In general, it is better for dual-earner couples to tend more toward the flexible side of the scale. Your marriage will experience less conflict and less stress, and you will grow together in your marriage as well as individually as you empower each other to pursue your interests and abilities outside the marriage.

Glen had been well trained for the professional world. He remembers being urged by his parents and teachers throughout his life to develop the skills and personal qualities that would ensure his success as a professional person. His wife, Janet, was also urged to develop personal qualities and skills to ensure success in her future profession—housewife and mother. She learned the art of creating a warm and supportive home environment for her husband and children. Glen and Janet had a traditional marriage founded on complementary roles.

Much to their dismay, Glen had a serious heart attack at age forty. Fortunately, Janet secured a job that utilized her college degree, and she had excellent opportunities to advance through a progressive promotional system. Glen remained at home, taking primary responsibility for the care of their high schoolers and doing part-time computer work from his home office.

Glen and Janet were both highly adaptable. Each utilized their respective personal qualities to adjust to the new roles required by this unexpected event. Looking back, they see how their transition to a dual-earner marriage was facilitated by their adaptability. They both were willing to relinquish the traditional roles in which they began their marriage and make the necessary adjustments.

Glen and Janet had to adapt permanently to new circumstances, but there may be certain times and circumstances in life that will require adaptability on a temporary basis. The Jones family experienced this when Carol spent a month in intensive training for her job promotion. Her husband, Scott, took up the slack of household and childcare responsibilities while she was focused on her work. In the end, her new promotion gave her more time with her husband and family. The entire family reaped the rewards of Scott and Carol's adaptability.

Are You Compatible in Your Ability to Adapt?

To understand how compatible you are in adapting to new roles, refer back to the exercise on pp. 122–23 and compare your total scores with your spouse's. As a rule of thumb, the greater the difference between your two scores, the less compatibility you have in your ability to adapt to new roles. If your two total scores differ by seventeen points or more, you need to pay special attention to how these differences in your ability to adapt are causing conflict and stress and threatening to pull your marriage apart. If the difference between your two scores is from eight to sixteen points, you are moderately compatible but need to determine how you can find more agreement in this area. If the difference between your total scores is less than eight, you are highly compatible, likely to find role sharing easy and even pleasurable, and don't experience much conflict over roles.

Couples who are compatible in their ability to adapt tend to work together to find life situations that are satisfying to both. This involves the ability to compromise and negotiate and to find win-win solutions for the big and small decisions you make in life. You may have to ask: Who's going to gain from the decision that we make? In what ways? Is this decision going to be for my career advantage or yours? Maybe you will make a decision one time because it is good for the husband. Next time you will make a decision that is to the wife's advantage.

When Jack was offered a position at Fuller Theological Seminary in Pasadena, things seemed like they were going to be a lot more advantageous for Jack than for

Judy. We talked long and hard about making a move, and Judy was willing to compromise—to leave a satisfying practice for the sake of a good career opportunity for Jack. Jack, compatible in his desire to adapt, made Judy's needs clear in his negotiations with the seminary. He said, "It's very important for me that Judy has opportunities and happiness here." As a result, Fuller opened a position for Judy.

While Judy still didn't know if she was going to like it or find the same satisfaction she had in her current position, she took the risk of moving to Pasadena knowing that it was important to Jack. What she thought was going to be a loss for her and a gain for Jack turned out to open up a vast array of new possibilities and opportunities for growth that she never would have anticipated. Because we were compatible in our willingness to adapt to a move and a new situation, we created a situation that was advantageous to us both.

It is also true that a couple's compatibility might lead them to adapt in an entirely different way. Not long ago, a promising young couple came to interview at Fuller. The seminary wanted to hire the husband and helped search for a position for the wife, too. Since there was nothing available that was satisfying for her, the couple decided not to accept the offer. In this case, the husband was willing to be adaptable enough to turn down a tempting offer because the move would not have been advantageous to his wife's career.

When you are compatible in your ability to adapt, you work together to do what is best for *both* spouses. When you are each willing to adapt to circumstances, you strengthen your commitment and maintain the cohesion that keeps your dual-earner careers from pulling you apart.

Flexibility

Dual-earner partners who adapt to new roles must also be flexible in how you carry out those roles. When you and your spouse share roles and responsibilities in the home, there are two aspects of flexibility that become important. The first is your ability to allow for interchangeability. Interchangeability means that spouses can switch roles or responsibilities at one point in a day, in a week, in a month, or in the marriage. In a dual-earner marriage, it isn't always the wife who picks the children up after school—sometimes the husband does. It isn't only one spouse who is responsible for having a meal on the table at the end of the day. When neither of you wants to scrub the toilet, you take turns—that's interchangeability.

Dual-earner couples also have to be flexible about standards. How flexible are you about how frequently the house gets cleaned? How flexible are you about the way it gets cleaned?

Elizabeth's large Hispanic family was relaxed about household order, but Fred, an only child, grew up in a home where everything was kept in its proper place. They were constantly irritated with each other over whose way was the right way, and their battles left them both feeling defeated and unloved. They got caught in a vicious blaming cycle that ended in stifling standoffs. Differences became irritations, irritations turned into anger, and anger led to resentment. Finally, they got a handle on their differences by looking together at how they rated on the adaptability scale. This gave them an idea of how flexible they each were. Elizabeth scored forty on the adaptability scale, and Fred scored ten.

For Elizabeth and Fred, improving their flexibility meant recognizing differences. They agreed that each of them had a different way of going about life and accomplishing tasks and that each held different beliefs about household work. They came to respect that each partner could be right but still do things differently. They recognized that, if they were to work together, they each needed to change—Fred needed to be more flexible in allowing for Elizabeth's more relaxed household standards, and Elizabeth needed flexibility to recognize and respect Fred's need for order.

When you are flexible, you give up judging and criticizing your spouse and become willing to admit that there's not only one way to do certain tasks in a dual-earner marriage. Flexibility allows saying to your spouse, "When you're in charge of the dishwasher, you can do it your way."

You can also let your differences work for you. You may decide to let the more structured spouse in your dual-earner marriage do the banking. The more visionary spouse is the one who plans the family fun nights and entertainment. Flexibility means recognizing your respective strengths and putting them to work for your mutual good.

Cohesion: How Together Should We Be?

Marital cohesion has to do with the degree of emotional closeness between you and your spouse and the degree of individual autonomy you experience in the marriage. In traditional, single-earner marriages, where there tend to be more complementary roles, each partner depends on the other for the particular role that partner assumes in the marriage. For example, in the conventional, single-earner marriage, the husband may depend on his wife to meet his social and emotional needs, while she depends on him for economic security. Such an arrangement assures a certain degree of cohesiveness (emotional closeness) in the marriage. However, the degree of cohesion may be so great that each spouse has little autonomy, since each needs the other to act as his or her complement in order to function. While it may appear that these spouses function independently in the marriage, in reality they each depend on the other.

In the dual-earner marriage, where work roles are separate and require that spouses function independently, you are less likely to depend on your spouse for the particular role he or she assumes in the marriage. While this arrangement can foster healthy autonomy, it can also make it more difficult for you to develop marital cohesion.

Dual-earner spouses can find it challenging to create marital cohesion. The pull of the husband's job and the pull of the wife's job almost guarantee that a husband and wife are going to be pulled apart from each other (see below).

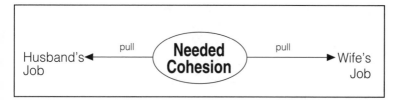

Being a dual-earner couple means that you have to work *intentionally* to develop cohesion. You have to take the time to establish and unite around a central meaning and purpose for your dual-earner marriage so that you won't be pulled apart.

Cohesion is what connects you in your roles. When you each have a sense of your shared meaning together, you can both be out in the work world, living independent, autonomous lives, but when you come home you experience a closeness and an interdependence because

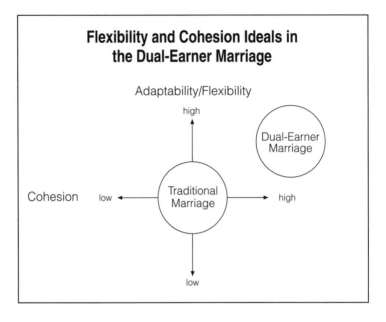

Flexibility and Cohesion Ideals in
the Dual-Earner Marriage

you are both agreed on your meaning together as a couple. Decisions about who buys the groceries, who does what chores around the house, and how you maintain a household and family are based on a commitment to making your new roles work for the good of the whole.

Cohesion can be doubly difficult for couples who are unhappy with their decisions about work. But even if you are a couple in which the wife is working because you need extra money but the arrangement goes against your ideal for marriage, you can still develop cohesion. You can unite around the purpose you've both agreed on. You've agreed you need the money; you've agreed the extra income is for your common good. Then, when you join forces to work together in the home, role sharing can become a blessing and not a curse.

Working together to create and balance new roles develops interdependence. Each partner is autonomous, capable of living independently of the other, but the two agree to work together to develop cohesion, uniting around a shared meaning and purpose.

Working Together

While traditional marriages can function with moderate amounts of adaptability/flexibility and cohesion because of their complementary roles, the dual-earner couple needs a higher amount of adaptability/flexibility and cohesion to make their new roles work (see previous page). As a dual-earner couple, you need to connect in your meaning, desires, and goals and find ways to work together to create new roles that enable you to fulfill your common meaning and purpose. You have to work intentionally to communicate, negotiate, compromise, and develop cohesion. When you do, you expand your capacity to come together and create deeper intimacy.

Part
4

Intimacy and Sex

10

Getting the Love You Need

Men want sex! Women want intimacy! Men tend to experience intimacy through sex, while women tend to desire to have sex when they experience their husband as being intimate. While this is an exaggeration, it speaks of the difficulty couples have when it comes to finding the love they need in their relationship. Finding this balance can be difficult in any marriage, but it is especially difficult in the busy lifestyle that dual-earner couples lead.

As a dual-earner couple, you are faced with the challenge of creating a relationship of personal closeness as you go about your separate, dual-earner lives together. To create an intimate relationship, you have to put as much time and energy into your marriage as you do into your work. You have to be intentional about making intimacy in your marriage central in your life.

Keeping Intimacy Alive

Intimacy will not develop on its own; you must build it into your marriage. With the challenge of creating new roles and the pull of two jobs, the potential for conflict and overload is high. At times it may even seem like work and work relationships are more appealing than home-life responsibilities and marriage. It is extremely important that you be *intentional* about creating intimacy: You must plan for intimate time together.

Think for a moment about your relationship with your spouse—your moments of intimacy, your sexual relationship. How many hours of the day do you spend thinking about your work or the next project you're going to do? When you come home ready to drop from your busy day, do you concentrate on being with your spouse that night?

What are your intimacy rituals? How can you create some if you don't already have them? Maybe you have them and you don't even think about them. When you first see each other at the end of the day, do you greet in some special way? Do you kiss? Do you talk? Do you ask what has happened at work during the day? Maybe you enjoy sitting down together and drinking a relaxing cup of tea, or reading a book, or going for a walk together. Whatever your rituals, it is important that you take the time to create and continue them.

In addition to your intimacy rituals, how else can you build and communicate intimacy? Intimacy between partners can be communicated in a number of ways: through body language, overt physical behavior, symbolic gestures, and written language. There may even be some truth that actions speak louder than words. Your eyes, lips, face, posture, and general body movement all do a great deal to express what you are feeling.

Generally, men and women specialize in different methods of communication. Women find it easier to express feelings in words, while men tend to express their feelings through actions.

Some men communicate intimacy through symbolic gestures, such as sending a bouquet of flowers, a single rose, or a card. It may be easier for men to express love in written form than to verbalize it. Love and appreciation can be expressed through a letter, poem, or song. Although they are disastrous as poetic art forms, Judy cherishes the love poems Jack has written to her. Intimacy in our marriage relationship can be renewed by such expressions of love.

But is the nonverbal form of communication, which men are often most comfortable with, sufficient? Can personal feelings of intimacy be communicated adequately in this way? Unfortunately for those men who find the verbal expression of intimacy so difficult, we believe that nonverbal communication lacks the combination of preciseness and personalness that is found in verbal modes of communication.

Nonverbal body language, overt physical behavior, and symbolic gestures may allow for personalness in communication, but they lack a degree of preciseness that characterizes verbal communication. Body language, for example, can be misread: *What does that gleam in his eye really mean?* Physical expressions can be misinterpreted: *Is he interested in me as a person or just my body?* Symbolic expressions may be questioned: *Why did he send me these flowers? What has he done now?* Although a high degree of precision is obtained in written communication, it is not always very personal. Expressing feelings with pen and paper doesn't allow for a simultaneous exchange of communication. In fact, these written expressions are usually intended to be read while the writer is not present.

We are not suggesting that verbal communication cannot also be misinterpreted. We are suggesting that intimate feelings of love and tenderness can be communicated most completely, personally, and precisely by verbal means. The expression of these feelings by both partners can have dramatic effects on your marital relationship. It can deepen and grow a relationship that has stagnated or grown distant and greatly increase the opportunities for a couple to mutually experience true intimacy.

Personal intimacy is so complex and multidimensional that it may be compared to a multifaceted diamond. A diamond can be appreciated from many angles, each one giving a different view of the unique beauty of the diamond. The depth and dimensions of personal intimacy are likewise best communicated in a variety of ways: body language, physical expressions, symbolic gestures, written word, and verbal communication. When you use multiple modes to express intimacy, you greatly expand your ability to express intimacy fully, heighten the sense of security each spouse has in the relationship, and build those moments of personal closeness essential to the creation of intimacy in a marriage.

Intimacy at Work

It is doubly important that dual-earner couples be intentional about creating and communicating intimacy. Spouses in a dual-earner marriage spend hours of time at work each day with coworkers of the opposite sex. The potential for opposite-sex intimacy in the workplace is great, and when you put so much time and effort into relationships at the workplace, you run the risk of meeting your intimacy needs through your coworkers. You spend the prime hours of the day with them, and maybe you enjoy that special person who consistently listens to you for an hour over lunch.

When you and your spouse come home exhausted from your work, there can be a temptation to think, *Ah, I'm going to work again tomorrow; I'll make my connection there.* There is also a danger that if all your time and energy in your dual-earner marriage is spent working out your conflicts and roles (deciding who is going to do the grocery shopping or house cleaning or dealing with the anger you might feel over your conflicting household roles), relationships at work will look very appealing.

Opposite-sex attractions in the workplace are natural, but they can threaten the intimacy in your marriage. You must be careful to intentionally create times for intimacy with your spouse, establishing an intimate environment that you look forward to coming home to. (See chapter 11 for further discussion of opposite-sex attractions in the workplace.)

Your Sexual Relationship

Marital sexual expression is an important way to develop intimacy with a spouse. However, husbands and wives need to recognize that they may come at intimacy and sexuality differently. Men are socialized to regard sexual activity as a pleasure for its own sake. In fact, sexual desire, ability, and even conquest are often considered masculine attributes by our society. Society also teaches men that to be masculine is to not express tender emotions. So when a man marries and finds that an intimate marital role requires that he be able to share affection and share his feelings, both of which involve the ability to communicate and be expressive, he may be at a loss.

For women, on the other hand, sex is more often an expression of shared affection and emotional connection. The ability to relate, to communicate, and to be expressive are important components of her sexual experience. So when her spouse initiates sex without the emotional connection, she may be at a loss. Given our differences, how can couples overcome these barriers to enjoyable sexual interaction?

From a woman's perspective, cultivating openness to the sexual desires in herself is important. Even though for a woman sex is an expression of herself emotionally, if you never allow yourself to embrace yourself as a sexual being with sexual passions, you will not experience the fullness of your sexuality.

A woman often comes home from a busy day at work and then puts in a second shift at home. When she relaxes, the last thing she thinks about is feeling sexy. As a woman, it is important that you give yourself time to think about being affectionate and what kinds of touch you would enjoy, making yourself more aware of your sexuality. What if you took the time to watch something romantic on television, to read a Gothic novel, or to do something else to energize your passionate side? Can you develop some rituals that create a sensual atmosphere for you? For a woman, sensuality, like intimacy, can be intentionally nurtured.

Men, on the other hand, face the challenge of being open to emotional intimacy. A man quite quickly can think that sex would be nice tonight—just the act of intercourse. But a man can go beyond this response and say, "Sexuality is about my enjoyment and desire of sex, but it is also about this special person. How do I connect with her emotionally as well as physically?"

When does sex begin? It begins in how you engage with your wife. When you come home, do you go read the paper or turn on the television? Or do you give your wife a kiss and willingly take on your shared role in the home?

If you find yourself complaining that your wife is not sexually responsive, think about how you have interacted with her during the day. Have you connected with her in any way? From a woman's perspective, the openness to being sexual is tied in with this expression of connection and intimacy. In fact, the Hite report[9] shows that when men were asked what they liked about sex, they, too, said that they liked the warmth and the security—the connection—of the sexual relationship. Maybe as a man you don't have to think so intentionally about being a sexual being, but you must be intentional about acknowledging your own need for emotional connection and communicating those needs to your wife in order to create a passionate sexual connection.

God intends for married persons to enjoy each other sexually and to derive pleasure and happiness out of the totality of your relationship together. This is called person-centered sexuality. When a wife becomes more expressive of her sexual self, and when a husband becomes more expressive of his affectionate self, it helps to foster the person-centered connection that builds intimacy. Seeing your spouse as a beloved person brings a depth to the intimate encounter of sexual intercourse. The sexual act can become more than just two bodies coming together with pleasant physical sensations, which are in themselves wonderful and a gift from God. It can become two people giving themselves to each other and coming together in a union that is, in a sense, mystical. This mystical union is the one-flesh union that is expressed in an intimate, person-centered connection when two people have a sense of common meaning and purpose. This strong, person-centered connection is a part of what keeps passion alive.

Keeping Sexual Passion Alive

Without your being aware of it, you and your spouse's attempt to juggle two jobs and a home life may have cut into the richness of your sexual relationship. In dual-earner marriages, where time and energy are often in short supply, you can come back to the principles of *commitment, forgiveness, empowerment,* and *intimacy* as foundations for keeping sexual passion alive.

Commitment

The foundation for a good sexual relationship is a marriage based on a mutual covenant commitment. Partners who feel secure in their commitment to one another will be more responsive sexually. A woman especially is most able to invest herself in a sexual relationship when she feels secure about the relationship. In the same way, a woman who does not trust her husband or has fears that she may lose him or be rejected by him is less able to enjoy an adequate sexual response. A man also seems to benefit from security in sexual intimacy with his wife, as he reports it makes him feel warm, trusted, and affirmed in his masculinity. When security is lacking in a relationship, there is a tendency for the sexual aspects of the relationship to deteriorate. Security and trust in a relationship are essential for sexual responsiveness and authenticity between the partners.

Marital sexuality will be most fulfilling when it is based on mutuality.

The wife's body does not belong to her alone but also to her husband. In the same way, the husband's body does not belong to him alone but also to his wife. Do not deprive each other except by mutual consent and for a time, so that you may devote yourselves to prayer. Then

come together again so that Satan will not tempt you
because of your lack of self-control.

2 Corinthians 7:4–5

The mutual consent in this verse indicates that the
couple must agree together through an awareness of
their equality and interdependence. "By mutual consent"
is a translation of the Greek phrase *ek symphōnou*, which
literally means "with one voice" (compare the English
word *symphony*). There is no room for the misguided
view that the husband initiates and dominates while the
wife unwillingly submits. The assumption in this
Scripture is that both partners desire sexual expression.
When you communicate in sensitive ways about your
sexual desires, you can reach a sexual harmony through
the mutuality of two unique persons expressing and
responding to each other's sexual needs and desires.

God pronounced what was created as good and
acceptable! A mutual covenant commitment invokes a
mutual acceptance of ourselves as special beings. When
you embrace sexuality as a gift of God, you are comfortable with your sexuality and body image. You have no
need to hide your sexual feelings and desires. Enjoy a
positive attitude about your entire body, including the
erogenous zones.

If you have trouble accepting your sexuality, you may
try to show signs of interest and then act disinterested
when your partner responds. An important aspect of
accepting your own sexuality is recognizing that each
spouse is independently responsible for his or her own
sexuality and sexual responsiveness. This means that
you don't blame your spouse when you experience a lack
of responsiveness. Rather, the unresponsive spouse
needs to take ownership and discover ways to increase
his or her own sexual receptivity. Obviously, if the relationship is pained and hurting on other levels of intimacy,

spouses need to address the impact that this is having on the lack of responsiveness. If you care enough about the relationship to bring things out into the open and take responsibility for what needs changing, you can renew the possibility of positive sexual responsiveness.

It is true that your mind often has more to do with your ability to respond sexually than your body does. It is important that you be in tune with your own sexuality and arousal potential so that you can draw on this knowledge and find ways to stay sexually responsive. What you tell yourself and how you prepare yourself sexually affects your openness to your partner as well as your own willingness to initiate a sexual approach. While all couples will have periodic difficulty with sexual arousal, regular sexual activity and functioning is generally conducive to satisfying sexual involvement. Accepting God's good creation of sexuality in yourself and your spouse will lead to personal and mutual expression of yourself in sexual intimacy.

Forgiveness

Couples need to practice the art of forgiveness in their sexual relationship. Sometimes you will disappoint your spouse and make mistakes that are hurtful to him or her and to your relationship. When you assume an attitude of forgiving and being forgiven, you take the edge off of the disruptions that certain blunders, differences, and misunderstandings cause.

The act of extending forgiveness involves accepting differences. Differences between spouses are inevitable and must be addressed in a marital relationship. It is important to remember that two becoming one flesh does not eradicate the individual. Marital sexuality entails the coming together of two people who are unique in their own sexuality. It is essential you appreciate and value your spouse's personal sexual value system.

Personal and gender sexual values are developed through early childhood experiences and attitudes learned from the family, church, and community. You each have personal preferences concerning such matters as sexual practices, values, standards, desires, frequency of sexual activity, and so on. For example, you may express a desire for a sexual expression that your spouse is uncomfortable with. In this case, you need to be understanding and listen to your spouse's personal value system and the deep feelings it may provoke. Within the safety of covenant love, you have the freedom to discuss these very personal matters. It will be necessary and appropriate for both of you to grapple together with these different values and the effect they have on your sexual relationship.

When trying to come to a mutual decision about your sexual practices, it will be essential to listen to your spouse's point of view and try to understand the differences. Sometimes you will relinquish a sexual request for the sake of your spouse, and other times it will be appropriate for your spouse to reevaluate his or her value system for your sake. In an intimate sexual relationship, both spouses are committed to each other and to working for the good of the relationship and for a loving resolution that is right for you as a couple and as individuals.

Spouses who put a priority on forgiveness will find ways to work out differences in their sexual relationship, and this will greatly benefit their sexual intimacy. When you have given each other negative or mixed messages about sexuality, when mistakes have been made or confusion arises out of your differences, forgiveness is that ingredient of grace that keeps you in a helpful and hopeful growth process.

Extraordinary understanding is necessary if your spouse has experienced a traumatic sexual encounter or abusive sexual situation. Such experiences can cause serious damage and distortions, and the victim will often repress or deny his or her sexuality as a protective measure. Grace (acceptance and forgiveness) will allow for the time and create the environment in which healing is possible, leading to sexual wholeness and restoration for your spouse.

Empowerment

Spouses must empower each other in the mutual giving and receiving of physical pleasure in the lovemaking experience. The ability for you and your spouse to be open and receptive to each other in a tender interaction of sexual pleasuring is not only mutually satisfying, but it also builds a sense of well-being in each of you and can be an empowering process.

Healthy, well-functioning sexual relationships are ones in which both partners view sexual activity as natural and something to be enjoyed together. When a couple's marital sexual satisfaction increases, each partner's general level of individual pleasure also increases. The mutual, active enjoyment of being erotically attracted to and stimulated by your spouse is gratifying to the ego and empowering. When you are keenly aware of your partner's preferences and unique value systems when giving and receiving pleasure, you will enhance each other's responsiveness.

There will be natural times of ebb and flow in sexual arousal and desire in marriage. The pressures of work combined with the additional demands of childcare responsibilities, household tasks, and health problems can temporarily diminish sexual responsiveness. The wife who works all day, comes home to fix the evening meal, and then cleans the house for three hours is not likely to be sexually responsive when she flops dead tired into bed. The husband who has worked long hours on a demanding job or who is anxious about the possibility of being fired experiences diminished sexual functioning. These dry spells require patience, restraint, and support so that you can empower each other to be responsive once again.

Good sexual functioning takes time, energy, and commitment. When you make your relationship a priority, stay flexible in the ebb and flow of sexuality, and bring an attitude of grace and empowering to the relationship, you enhance your intimacy and your sexual passion.

Marital sexuality involves much more than physical intercourse, however. It is important that spouses empower each other by giving and receiving emotionally as well as physically. Our alertness to feelings of closeness and intimacy in nonsexual ways is a reciprocal process. It is extremely important that you and your spouse communicate verbally and nonverbally your expressions of tenderness, affection, understanding, desire, warmth, comfort, and excitement. When you and your spouse take time to communicate and touch each other in emotional and physical ways, you invite an emotional responsiveness that empowers each partner's intimacy.

Intimacy

The self-esteem and well-being your spouse will feel in the comfort and joy of simply being embraced by you will bring about a time of deepest intimacy for the two of you. The deep sense of vulnerability and love that occurs between partners in reciprocal emotional sharing leads to deeper levels of intimacy. This involves a mutual submissiveness in which one partner gives priority to the other's needs, while expressing his or her own needs as well, so that there is opportunity for a giving and receiving interaction. Serving and being served is a mutually empowering process that can deepen the love and respect between you and your spouse. This is an important part of sexual intimacy.

Spouses need to communicate their sexual feelings and desires to each other. You need to know what your partner desires sexually, and your partner needs to know the same, without having to play a guessing game. Sexual desire is often communicated nonverbally, but it is important that the communication be verbalized as well. You and your spouse need to find your own special way, and the appropriate time, to communicate about your sexual relationship so the thoughts and needs that are expressed can be received and responded to.

Guiding each other through touch and short words of encouragement during lovemaking can be a helpful way to communicate sexually. However, it is also essential that you take special time that is not during lovemaking to talk together about your sexual relationship. It is useful to periodically evaluate how each of you feels about your sexual relationship and to address dissatisfactions so you can make any needed adjustments. This is often difficult for couples to put into practice, but if differences are not addressed, you will tend to take on more dysfunctional patterns of dissatisfaction.

Discussing your sexual interaction openly with each other will help you find positive ways to improve and/or reinforce the things that are contributing positively to your sexual relationship. You should expect areas of disagreement, since both you and your spouse came to your relationship with your own personal sexual value systems. These values need to be honored and carefully understood as you work together to find a mutually satisfactory solution.

Finally, an element of involvement is an important part of sexual interaction. One way to be involved is to create a fun and playful responsiveness. Playfulness occurs when you are able to let go of self-consciousness or embarrassment about nudity and sexual involvement. This reflects your God-given ability to be physically naked and not ashamed. Honest communication and a healthy view of your sexual self and your body are vital ingredients of being free to enter into a playful sexual encounter.

The other crucial part of involvement is the ability to personally give of yourself freely and without fear—to be unabashedly responsive to your spouse with body, mind, and soul. If you are comfortable with yourself sexually and are not self-conscious during lovemaking, you will be free to respond with your whole being.

Partners who assume a spectator role during coitus are those who become self-conscious in how they are performing or looking to themselves or the other. They tend to remove themselves from the scene and are spectators rather than participating in the lovemaking. When this happens, a person becomes so focused on the performance that it inhibits spontaneous personal sexual responses.

We live in a technologically oriented society that emphasizes the importance of using the right technique. This may lead some to reduce intimacy to little more than an exercise of techniques. When this happens, sex begins to resemble the once popular paint-by-number kits. Following the specific instructions of a sex manual on every detail leaves the couple with a set of rules or techniques that dictate their lovemaking. Just picture the scenario in which the wife turns to the husband and says, "Turn back a page, honey! We must have missed a step, because

I'm not enjoying this." The outcome is unsatisfactory because there has been no creative personal interaction between the spouses. In a very real sense, the person-hood of each spouse has been lost in the effort to make love by the book. The intimate response between the lover and the beloved has been replaced by an effort to be technically correct.

When you separate yourself from sexual involvement, you focus on your role as lovemaker and fail to be involved in the lovemaking experience itself. This removal of self in the sexual event is invariably self-defeating because it reduces the personal intimacy and interactional experience. Authentic sexuality requires that you freely and naturally express feelings, inclinations, and actions with your partner.

Good marital sex occurs when partners are spontaneously involved as active participants in the encounter and are able to lose themselves in the moment. It is a reciprocal giving and receiving activity that increases the one-flesh complementary union.

When you have a strong foundation in your relationship—covenant love that allows you to trust the commitment, an atmosphere of forgiveness that allows you to experience and accept your differences, and mutual empowerment and meaning—then you can be open and vulnerable emotionally and sexually with each other. You can go to a deeper level of intimacy and a more passionate expression of sexuality, which counteracts the tendency of the dual-earner marriage to pull you apart and erode intimacy.

When you are working together on all levels of meaning and purpose as a couple and have a strong sense of being called into a marriage where God brings about a one-flesh union, intimacy can go beyond you as a couple and back out into the world. This can energize you in your work, and it can give you a greater capacity to be present for your spouse and children in appropriate ways. This is God's intention in creating man and woman for this one-flesh union. You can find a shared meaning and purpose and deepen the intimacy in your marriage in the midst of the pressures and stresses of the dual-earner marriage.

11

Opposite-Sex Friendships

Can't We Just Be Friends?

When men worked outside of the home and women worked mainly in the home, there was little opportunity outside of family relationships for men and women to get to know each other very well. Few women could say, "Some of my closest friends are men," nor could many men say, "Some of my closest friends are women."

Things have changed! Women and men work side by side, often on an equal basis, eight hours a day, five days a week. Women and men now have the opportunity to get to know each other in a way that was not possible in the past. For unmarried persons, the change has made it easier to meet an eligible opposite-sex person.

For spouses in dual-earner marriages, however, there are some unique considerations that must be addressed when an opposite-sex friendship develops at the workplace. One is the fear that an emerging friendship may develop into a romantic or sexual relationship. A recent statistic justifies such a fear. In half of the divorces now taking place, one of the spouses is already romantically involved with someone else before the divorce occurs. As a result, when supportive nonromantic and nonsexual opposite-sex friendships do emerge, spousal jealousy often demands that this relationship be terminated.

What's Possible and What's Desirable?

Is it possible for members of a dual-earner marriage to develop close, nonromantic, nonsexual friendships with persons of the opposite sex? You must begin by realizing that in a certain sense, any relationship between two members of the opposite gender is a sexual relationship—be it between mother and son, father and daughter, or sister and brother. Your sexual identity is a part of who you are. You can't divorce yourself from it, and therefore any relationship includes your sexual self. The fact that this is so can cause you to be very fearful and can create a barrier to the development of close and meaningful relationships with members of the opposite sex.

Even so, it is possible. Your ability to enjoy a close and meaningful, even intimate friendship with someone of the opposite sex while refraining from romantic or sexual involvement will, of course, depend on a number of factors, not the least of which is the nature of each person's marital relationship. In addition, it will depend on your ability to establish and respect guidelines for an opposite-sex friendship that assumes a proper place relative to your marriage relationship.

Is it desirable for members of a dual-earner marriage to develop close friendships at work with persons of the opposite sex? Yes, they can be a source of rich human experiences, an avenue for challenging and fulfilling intellectual exchange, and they can serve to strengthen the marriage relationships of the friends who engage in them.

Since close opposite-sex friendships are both possible and desirable, the question is, how can these friendships be established? Intimacy with someone of the opposite sex is potentially explosive. Your sexual orientation and identity influence how you relate to those of the opposite sex. When an attractive man and an attractive woman become close friends, it can be expected that sexual feelings will begin to emerge. For this reason, most people handle the potential of opposite-sex entanglement by avoidance.

However, to use avoidance exclusively as a way to prevent extramarital encounters would be an impossibility in our society. Furthermore, it would be a regression rather than a constructive solution to a very real problem—the risk of developing illegitimate opposite-sex friendships.

Mike and Sue Irwin are in their thirties. They are fairly well adjusted in their marriage, and have three elementary-school-age children. Sue, who works full-time in a large insurance firm, became friends with a man at work—Bill Jordan. Bill and Ellen Jordan are also in their thirties. They have two lovely children, and their marriage is basically sound, with only the typical types of disagreements. With Mike's consent, Sue invited Bill and his family over for a backyard barbecue, and their families really hit it off. Since then, they had been to each other's homes numerous times and recently spent a weeklong vacation together at the beach.

The families got along beautifully together, with the usual amount of teasing that goes on between friends. Mike, although good-natured, is a more serious type than

Bill. Though Sue is in love with her husband, Mike, she began to admit to herself that she really liked the way Bill teased her and his enthusiastic approach to life. In fact, she found herself quite attracted to Bill and flirtatiously sought out his attention. She sensed he was attracted to her from the vibes between them.

Sue's feelings and flirtatious behavior began to bother her. She asked herself the frightening question, *Could I be falling in love with another man?* She was sure of her love for Mike but confused and scared by the attraction she felt toward Bill.

In reaction, Sue started to avoid Bill at the office. One day Mike suggested they ask Bill and Ellen to go with them to a movie. He was somewhat surprised when she suggested that maybe they should get to know Steve and Julie Anderson more and asked them instead. From that point on, the Irwins and Jordans saw less and less of each other, since Sue usually found some excuse about why they could not be together. When Sue was offered a transfer to another department in the insurance firm, she eagerly accepted. She never did talk to her husband, Mike, about her attraction for Bill, and she most certainly did not discuss the situation with Bill and Ellen. She handled her attraction for Bill by simply avoiding contact altogether.

Avoidance is one way out of a dilemma, but it unfortunately involves a cost. In this case, it cost the Irwins and Jordans a potentially close relationship with each other as families. Perhaps it was the right decision in the long run, but because out of fear Sue avoided a situation she didn't understand rather than facing up to it with her husband, she set an unhealthy pattern.

Avoidance is a common way people solve potential conflict situations. In fact, entire cultures try to prevent romantic entanglement between members of the opposite sex by simply prohibiting interaction between them. In the Near East, Muslim societies traditionally have allowed no opposite-sex friendships outside of the immediate family. The only females a man can expect to be close to in an entire lifetime are his mother, his sister, and his wife. A woman can have no friendships with men except for her father, her brother, and her husband. The whole purpose behind the veiling of women is to prevent any nonfamilial intimacy between men and women. Women are thought to have an almost irresistible power over men because of their sexuality. Men are thought to be rendered powerless over their sexual urges in the presence of a woman who does not cover her sexuality—her legs, arms, and face. Muslims believe that *fitna* or chaos would result in society if women and men were allowed the freedom to mix socially.

The solution is to allow no public contact between males and females. Muslim societies even differentiate space by sex. There is male space and female space. Any public area—the marketplace, roads, squares, and sidewalks—is male space. A female is forbidden to enter male space alone; she must either be with a group of women or be escorted by her husband, father, or brother. Private space is female space and is usually defined within the walls of a home. Males are not allowed to enter this female space unless a father, husband, or brother is present.

It's amazing to consider the extent a society goes to in order to prevent extramarital encounters. Fear of the power of sex seems to drive them to an extreme position of avoidance. We choose to believe there is a better way to deal with our sexuality in opposite-sex relationships. The guidelines in this chapter can give direction about healthy opposite-sex friendships. A close opposite-sex friendship is possible when:

- The relationship has intellectual, emotional, and psychological levels, but not a physical level.
- Commitment will be given to the friendship as long as it remains nonthreatening and secondary to the primary marital relationship of each friend.

Levels of Opposite-Sex Friendships

There are several levels on which a relationship between a man and a woman can operate. In the marriage relationship, the husband and wife share themselves with each other on every level—intellectual, emotional, physical. In an opposite-sex friendship, it is important to realize the limitations of the relationship for each level.

Intellectual Level

One of the greatest unrealistic and unnecessary burdens that you can place on your marriage relationship is the expectation that your spouse will fulfill all of your needs. If you expect your spouse to be all things to you, your spouse will feel inadequate when he or she can't meet all of your needs or feel jealous when someone else is better able to fulfill one dimension of your needs.

In our modern society, each working spouse is likely to be involved in a very specialized form of work. In the past, when the majority of families were agrarian, both husband and wife were involved in the same type of economic activity. But today, because of occupational specialization, husbands and wives often have very little knowledge about the details of their spouse's occupation. Because of occupational specialization, a high degree of intellectual sharing is possible in opposite-sex friendships. It is within our occupational tasks that many of our creative energies gain expression. We admire and are drawn to others in our occupation who possess creative energies similar to our own.

Rhonda is a counselor working for the Forest City counseling center. She is happily married to her husband, Ken, and they have three children. Brent works at the counseling center with Rhonda, and he and Rhonda often do cotherapy counseling. Brent has been happily married to his wife, Nancy, for eight years. Although Rhonda and Brent are both committed to their spouses, they spend a lot of time together at the center and have grown very close to each other. They enjoy working together, appreciate the intellectual stimulation they give each other, and find each other physically attractive.

Rhonda really admires the way Brent is able to conduct group counseling, and he recognizes how skilled she is in working with children. They spend much time together talking about counseling at coffee breaks, over lunch, and even when they and their spouses get together. They may develop a mutual admiration, an understanding between them on the intellectual level that is not as fully developed with their spouses. Is there any danger in this?

The degree of intellectual intimacy that can develop between opposite-sex friends is dependent on the strength and health of the relationships between each friend and his or her spouse. If Rhonda's husband, Ken, happens to be a successful lawyer who is quite secure in his occupation and intellectual ability, he is not likely to be threatened by Rhonda's occupational sharing with Brent. On the other hand, if Ken is unsure of himself and struggling professionally, he may very well be resentful of the positive affirmation that Brent is receiving from Rhonda.

We are not suggesting that each spouse must be intellectually fulfilled by the other spouse in some academic way before they can tolerate an external intellectual intimacy on the part of their spouse. Let's suppose that Brent's wife, Nancy, completed her education at high school and then became a secretary before she met and married Brent. She now has three children in school and has returned to secretarial work. Nancy still finds time to lead a Girl Scout troop and teach the eighth-grade Sunday school class at church. She is creative in all her tasks and is receiving much positive reinforcement from others. Nancy is secure enough in herself that she is not threatened by Brent's professional intimacy with Rhonda. If the marriage relationships are secure, we see no limits in intellectual intimacy between opposite-sex friends.

Emotional Level

Emotional intimacy is the psychological and social dimension of a friendship. It involves two people feeling emotionally comfortable with each other so that they can disclose their thoughts, emotions, and lives without fear.

The extent to which opposite-sex friends will be able to become emotionally intimate will depend on the nature of their marriage relationships. As counselors, Rhonda and Brent are skilled in the art of human relating. They have developed empathetic skills, are trained to be sensitive to the needs and feelings of others, and know when and how to say a comforting or challenging word to other people. They are naturally able to get deeply connected emotionally as friends. However, if they get more intimate with each other than they do with their respective spouses, it raises another red flag because it puts the friendship in a priority over the marriage.

On the other hand, if the emotional intimacy between Rhonda and Brent is shared with their respective families and spouses, it can benefit everybody. Their emotional intimacy should allow them to see the other's spouse in the same light that they view their friend. They will be able to love and appreciate their friend's family members. In this type of emotional intimacy, the friendship is a contributing strength to the marriage relationships of each. Emotional intimacy should allow opposite-sex friendships to be complementary instead of competitive to marriage relationships. If Rhonda or Brent feels that either has a shortcoming in relating to their spouses, they can share this with each other, and by so doing help the other to develop into a more complete marriage partner.

Physical Level

There are very few close opposite-sex friendships in which each of you does not at least occasionally experience physical attraction or sexual desire. Your first reaction is often to deny the feelings because of the guilt and confusion they cause. Denial of feelings, however, is no solution and ultimately can only have harmful consequences to yourself, to your relationship with your friend, and to your relationship with your spouse.

When sexual feelings occur, the first thing you must do is to admit the feelings to yourself so you are openly aware of what is happening. The feelings themselves are not the problem but rather how you choose to deal with them. Feelings can be contained or acted on.

What is the best way to contain sexual feelings in a friendship? It is important to verbalize such attractions to your spouse. Doing this keeps you from guilt that might come from hiding these feelings.

One important guideline is that *nothing should be kept secret!* Your spouse needs to be aware of and be comfortable with your interaction with your opposite-sex friends. Is a bear hug in front of others or an arm around the shoulder acceptable? What forms of touch are acceptable when in private? When these matters are openly discussed, it shows respect for all parties to work together in trusting ways about the physical limits in a friendship. Some people are able to touch in natural and friendly ways, free of any sexual connotation. Other people are uncomfortable with giving or receiving touch. Such differences can be expected and must be thoroughly discussed.

Informing your spouse about your relationship with opposite-sex friends treats your spouse with respect and creates trust. Then you can discuss and agree together on appropriate guidelines for that particular friendship.

We cannot overemphasize the importance of making clear decisions about your friendship with someone of the opposite sex. The responsibility for establishing healthy guidelines rests first with you, then your spouse, and then the friend.

Opposite-Sex Friendships and Marriage

A close opposite-sex friendship is possible when commitment will be given to the friendship as long as it remains nonthreatening and secondary to the primary marital relationship of each friend. If intimacy were to be greater in the friendship than in either friend's marriage relationship, there would be a real danger that the marriage would become the secondary relationship. Opposite-sex friendships must always exist as secondary relationships and should be engaged in only by persons who already are part of a loving, meaningful, intimate marriage relationship.

Friends must be acutely aware of their own psychological needs and desires. They must be secure enough in their marriage so that they will not allow their friendship to develop into a primary relationship. If a spouse is not receiving sufficient emotional intimacy, if basic psychological and social needs are not being met in the marriage relationship, then the development of an intimate opposite-sex friendship is dangerous indeed. Opposite-sex friends should, at this point, decide to limit the friendship and establish a stronger relationship in the marriage.

Should opposite-sex friendships be avoided if you recognize that your own marriage has its shortcomings? Not necessarily, but you should be aware of your vulnerability when the friendship promises to become more intimate than your marriage.

Till Inconvenience Do Us Part

If you are fortunate enough to be a part of an intimate opposite-sex friendship, you must not get a false sense of its permanence. When you marry, you commit yourself to your spouse for life—"till death do us part." Your commitment to your opposite-sex friend will continue as long as it works and positively contributes to your marriage relationship. The friendship can end when one friend moves away, finds another job, or changes to a degree that can't be tolerated by the other.

Sometimes it will be necessary to give up an intimate friendship, and that is not easy. If this happens, you should view the intimacy of friendship as a positive force that has engendered personal growth and prepared you to establish this kind of intimate friendship in the future.

Some of you may be uncomfortable using the word *intimate* to describe an opposite-sex friendship, but the New Testament holds up such an ideal. In writing to Timothy, the apostle Paul advised him to treat "older women as mothers, and younger women as sisters, with absolute purity" (1 Tim. 5:2). It is significant that Paul chose examples of family relationships that are meant to be non-sexual yet intimate. A good rule of thumb is to seek to relate to your friend as you would to a member of your own family, with the same pure thoughts and intentions that you would have for your own sister, daughter, mother, brother, son, or father.

When you establish and respect certain principles and guidelines, the development of opposite-sex friendships is possible and desirable. When you are already part of a loving, meaningful, and intimate marriage relationship, you will find that your friendship can enrich your life and the lives of those around you. Opposite-sex friendships can be the source of rich human experiences and intellectual exchange. They can serve to strengthen your marriage and expand your capacity for intimacy and caring.

Part
5

Parenting

12

What Children Need from Dual-Earner Parents

In many dual-earner marriages, part of a couple's shared meaning is found in raising children. A couple may decide to add children to their family after they are well established in their dual-earner marriage. Other couples become dual-earners later in their marriages, after already having children. Either way, when a dual-earner marriage is also a dual-earner family, you face the challenge of incorporating an additional set of roles and responsibilities into your relationship. Not only must you as a couple consider how to share the responsibilities and demands of raising children, but you must also deal with how an already demanding dual-earner marriage affects your ability to be good-enough parents to your children.

167

The Benefits of Dual-Earner Parenting

In traditional single-earner families, most of the *parenting* is in reality *mothering*. We believe that one of the strengths of dual-earner homes can be a greater sharing of involvement by *both* a mother and a father in the lives of their children. Few parents can be all that they need to be to their children. But together, a mother and a father can complement each other by each being strong when the other feels weak and overextended. The important thing is that both parents be equally involved and bonded in the lives of their children. Although some experts fear that the dual-earner marriage is an invitation to child neglect, we believe that it can be turned into a benefit for children if fathers and mothers give equal priority to the needs of their children.

There has been an accumulation of recent evidence demonstrating the benefits of coparenting for children and parents alike. When both the father and mother are jointly involved in parenting, a family has what family therapists refer to as a strong parental subsystem: both father and mother take clear leadership when it comes to nurturing and guiding their children.

Recent research has shown that when compared to noncoparented children, coparented children:

- have a more secure sense of basic trust
- can more successfully adapt to brief separations from the mother
- have closer relationships to both mother and father
- develop better social discrimination skills, such as discerning who can best meet their needs
- display greater creativity and moral development
- have less animosity toward the other gender

- are better able to develop strong friendship bonds with opposite-sex children
- display fantasies of sustained connectedness[10]

Research also indicates that sons receive great benefits from coparenting. Sons who had a strong bond with both their father and mother were more able to display empathy, affection, and nurturing behavior, thought highly of the way they were parented, and were more likely to state that they wanted to be a father when they grew up.[11]

Girls who are coparented receive equal benefits—they show a greater sense of self and personal boundaries. Research shows that when a father, in particular, takes an active interest in his daughter's achievements, she is likely to succeed in her career goals.[12] Mothers who model assertiveness and self-confidence, in addition to nurturing behaviors, give their daughters permission to set firm boundaries as well as make emotional connections with others.

There is also abundant evidence that coparenting is a benefit to parents. If you are a working mother, you may receive the most obvious benefits. Coparenting should provide some relief from the reality that you often hold two jobs: one in the economic force and one at home. In addition, you will be less likely to be enmeshed or over-involved with your children.

If you are a father involved in the coparenting process, you will find that the socioemotional and relational sides of your personality develop. In contrast to the world of work outside the home, where decisions are expected to be based on the rational rather than the emotional, taking care of children inclines men to consider personal and emotional issues. This will not only change the way you relate in the home, but it can have a positive impact on the way you perform your work roles as well. Men who have high empathy skills can more effectively relate to other persons they must work with daily. Even organization management theory now stresses the need for personnel in the business world to understand the social and emotional needs of workers.

Coparenting allows mothers and fathers to better understand and be involved with their children and to be more consistent and effective in discipling them. As you coparent, dual-earner spouses will need to learn to complement each other as each relates to the children in his or her own way. Changing circumstances in your work situation may affect the relative amount of time each parent can spend with children. One parent may be better able to give more time when children are in their infancy or young childhood, while the other may be able to devote more time when the children are in high school.

Ideally, dual-earner parents need to find ways to complement each other on a day-to-day basis throughout your parenting years. Individual situations will determine which of your parental skills are most needed. While one parent may be more capable of helping a child with homework, the other may be more able to provide the encouragement needed when the child is discouraged and lacking in self-esteem. A strength in complementary parenting is that one parent does not have to attempt to meet all of the parenting needs of a child.

When you capitalize on the role-sharing reality of your dual-earner marriage, you can engage in *dual parenting*. You will find that the benefits will soon be realized by you, your spouse, your children, and in your dual-earner family life in general.

Good-Enough Parents

Some people strive to be perfect parents. There are at least two things wrong with this:

1. If you expect to be a perfect parent, you are holding up a standard for yourself that will only result in your being a failure in your own eyes.
2. Perfect parents can be too demanding of their children, not accepting them unless the children are perfect also.

Some of the popular writing on parenting too often gives the message that parents can have perfect children if they just parent the right way. Parenting books, complete with how-to formulas, promise that the right techniques will produce perfect children in the same way that skilled gardening produces beautiful flowers. However, what may work with flowers does not necessarily work with children.

Yet all parents, including dual-earner parents, need to be *good-enough parents*. Good-enough parents will do what they can for the good of their children, given the strengths and limitations of their circumstances. They know they will make mistakes and disappoint their children, but they will, nevertheless, be able to give the support and guidance that their children need. They will bond with their children in a way that is good enough to allow their children to develop and grow on their own.

Given the overload that many dual-earner parents experience, being good enough is sometimes difficult—but it is possible. It is important that dual-earner parents concentrate less on the how-tos of good parenting and more on the process of *being* a parent. Good parenting is a matter of interacting with your children in day-in, day-out living experiences that build your relationship with your children. Put aside your how-to-parent books and simply become a real person to your children. Even though these how-to materials can offer useful guidelines that can contribute to an understanding of the parenting process, you can function more freely and openly in your

parenting role if you are simply willing to be more genuine with your children.

God, the Good Parent

What does a good-enough parent look like? The best
model can be found in what Scripture tells of the way God
parents. Myron Chartier describes seven attributes of
God's love that show us what good-enough parenting
involves.[13]

1. *God cares for people.* Although this is preeminently
   demonstrated in the incarnation, death, and resurrection of Christ, numerous biblical passages
   stress the caring nature of God (see Luke 15:11–32;
   1 Peter 5:7).
2. *God is responsive to human needs.* We see this in the
   covenant God established after the flood (see Gen.
   9:8–17), in God's rescuing of Israel from Egypt (see
   Deut. 32), and in God's freely giving grace, mercy,
   and restoration (see John 3:16; Titus 3:3–7).
3. *God reveals love by giving.* God gave his only Son
   (John 3:16) and the power to become his children
   (John 3:1–2). He also gave us the Holy Spirit as our
   Comforter (John 14:16–17).
4. *God shows respect.* This is an attitude of considering the importance of the other person as someone
   valued and cherished who is free to be rather than
   being dominated or possessed.
5. *God knows us.* His Son was made in human likeness
   (see John 1:14; Phil. 2:5–8; Heb. 2:17–18; 4:15), and
   his knowledge of us penetrates to the core of our
   existence (see Ps. 44:21; John 2:25).
6. *God forgives us* (see Ephesians 1:7; John 3:17; Heb.
   4:15–16).

7. *God disciplines us as an expression of love* (see Prov. 3:11–12; Heb. 12:5–8; Rev. 3:19). The discipline God exercised over Israel can be seen as an attempt to create a faithful and obedient people.

Taken as a whole, the biblical emphasis is clearly placed on the love and grace that God so freely gives. However, this is not a watered-down type of easy love, empty of expectations or without demands. God's love includes disciplinary action that is meant for the good of the one being disciplined. God's parental love bears a striking similarity to the social science literature that points to the importance of high *parental support* and high *parental control*.[14] The actions of God model a parenting style in which parental love (support) and discipline (control) intertwine in encouraging a developing maturity in children.

Parenting Styles

You can lay aside the notion that you have to be a perfect parent and that there is only *one* correct way to develop perfect children. With God as your model, you can take a realistic look at what children of dual-earner parents need and how dual-earner parents can be good-enough parents. While some parenting styles encourage growth and are empowering, others hinder or block growth either by fostering dependency or by expecting self-reliance prematurely.

Early attempts to understand parenting styles made a distinction between *permissive* versus *restrictive* parenting. Proponents of the permissive style, while not rejecting the need for discipline, stressed that a child's greatest need is for warmth and security. Those holding to the restrictive style, while not rejecting parental affection, emphasized that a child's greatest need is for discipline, responsibility, and self-control.

In hundreds of studies done on parenting styles over the last thirty years, two factors—parental control and parental support—have emerged as the most important elements in good parenting. The term *parental control* means that you, as a parent, actively provide guidelines, set limits, direct and redirect your child's behavior in some desired direction. The term *parental support* refers to the affirmation, encouragement, and general support that you give to assure your children that they are accepted and cared for.

A variety of parenting styles can emerge when you combine differing degrees of control and support in parenting your children (see below). The four alternative parenting styles—neglectful, authoritarian, permissive, and authoritative—are generalizations or caricatures of what parenting is like in that particular style. No one style may be truly representative of the way you, or any one person, engage in parenting. As you read the description for each of the four parenting styles, remember that your style may

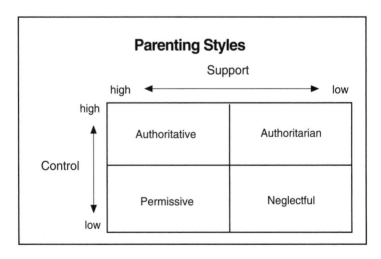

best be represented anywhere within the grid, including at the very center.

Neglectful Parenting

The neglectful parenting style is the easiest to criticize because it is obviously not good enough. The primary negative effect of a parenting style in which there is low support and low control is that there is very little bonding between parents and children. It is important to acknowledge, however, that because of the amount of time they must spend away from the home, dual-earner parents are particularly susceptible to using this style. The latchkey child, who is given a key to the house to lock himself or herself in when parents are away at work, is a casualty of neglectful parenting. Dual-earner parents sometimes have little choice and agonize over the fact that there is not adequate time for providing support or control when so many other demands are made on them.

Mary is a junior high art teacher, and her husband, Phil, works as an insurance broker at a nearby office. Some nights and weekends Mary must be at school for special events while, on occasion, Phil must call on customers in the evenings or on weekends. In their absence Devan, their son, has taken to watching television and videos, becoming more and more withdrawn. His special events often go unnoticed by his parents or are marred when one or both of them breaks a promise to attend. Devan gives the briefest of answers to their questions when they are home and has begun shutting them out of his life in order not only to protect himself but also to act out his anger passive-aggressively.

When work leaves little time for parenting and you adopt the neglectful parenting style, it can be tempting to rationalize that children benefit by being on their own. Such parents may even downplay the need to teach values and morals to their children, arguing that children need to experiment and come to their own conclusions about personal values. Such a philosophy emphasizes a child's right to the freedom to discover his or her own beliefs and lifestyle, and suggests that character is built by allowing children to make their own way in the world.

Dual-earner parents who succumb to this idea of parenting will reap what family therapists refer to as family disengagement. In disengaged families, members' lives rarely touch each other in any meaningful way. Such an autonomous family style is characteristic of many urban families in which both parents are working away from the home.

Christopher Lasch believes that when there is no authority figure in the home, the child becomes a ready victim for an authoritarian leader, group, or cult that preys on such neglected young people.[15] Indeed, some recent literature suggests that recruits to authoritarian-oriented religious cults come from neglectful homes. It is these individuals who seem to be hungry for a strong and strict leader to follow and obey without question. Such people are most susceptible to the dictates of an authoritarian figure, largely because they have never experienced a bonding with any authority figure in their own upbringing. Children raised in such a setting seem to lack any type of developed superego, the internalized set of external societal rules that serves as a guide and rule for their own behavior.

Authoritarian Parenting

Joyce is a lawyer in a large law firm, and Syd is a stock-broker. They have one son, Sean, in elementary school, and one daughter, Lisa, in junior high school. Joyce and

Syd expect their daughter to take care of Sean and demand strict adherence to many household rules. They abdicate their role as parents on many occasions, and Lisa is overburdened with adult responsibility. As she progresses in school and develops an interest in activities and friends outside of her family, Lisa resents these demands and wants to be set free. Joyce and Syd tell her that their way is the only way while she lives in their home.

When parents practice an authoritarian parenting style, the focus is on obedience and following the rules. Little time or attention is spent meeting the children's needs for nurture. Children reared within such homes are likely to be respectful and obedient to their parents, but they lack warmth, openness, or intimacy.

Dual-earner parents who can't always be present to give the type of support their children need may be tempted to make up for this by becoming more authoritarian. While this parenting style may tend to bind children to the family with *shoulds, oughts,* and *supposed tos,* because of the lack of emotional bonding between parent and child, there is little else to hold such a relationship together.

Permissive Parenting

Parents who, because their lives are too busy, fail to give their children the control and guidance they need are especially vulnerable to the permissive style. In its ideological form, permissive parenting is based on the assumption that a child is born like a rosebud, needing only tender love and support in order to blossom slowly into a beautiful flower. The present-day permissive parenting style has its roots in the ideals of the counterculture movement. The movement's philosophy said that every child has special potentialities at birth, and societal rules and standards destroy these natural tendencies. Therefore, children need to be allowed to find their own purpose through free expression: "Do your own thing."

Noticeably absent in the permissive parenting style is the idea that children tend to be quite self-centered and need parental guidance in learning values and interaction skills. Children raised in permissive homes tend either to lack social responsibility or to develop a strong sense of independence.

Authoritative Parenting

Authoritative parents combine the best qualities found in the partially adequate authoritarian and permissive parental styles. The authoritative parenting style tends to be the most effective and the most true to God's model because it succeeds in combining the parenting methods and traits necessary for raising happy, competent children.

One of the best-documented findings on parenting is that socially competent children are products of homes in which the parenting style is authoritative.[16] Children who possess social competence demonstrate self-esteem, academic achievement, cognitive development, creativity, an internal locus of control, moral behavior (such as honesty and trustworthiness), and the ability to do tasks on their own (such as eating, dressing, and caring for themselves).

Jay and Stacy are good examples of the authoritative parenting style. A typical interaction in their household looks something like this: Jay and Stacy arrive home from work to find their daughter, Dora, engrossed in afternoon cartoons. After greeting one another, Stacy asks Dora if she's started her homework. Dora sighs and says she will after the cartoons. Stacy reminds Dora that she knows the rules—homework before play. She also tells Dora she'll be finishing up some office work while Dad fixes supper. After supper they'll all be able to enjoy a favorite family television show. Stacy gives Dora a hug as they walk to their desks to get their work done so they can be free to enjoy supper and family time together later. Jay tells Dora he'll be glad to help her with her homework while he's working in the kitchen. Theirs is a busy household where both warmth and structure help its members thrive.

The Importance of Teaching and Modeling in Coparenting

Support and guidance are the two dimensions of parenting that give our children the security they need to become responsible persons. Much of what our children learn from us is caught through what we model as well as taught through what we say about the values we espouse. In some homes, children are left on their own to find reasons for their beliefs or good models for their behavior because their parents neglect the teaching role or model behaviors that are inconsistent with what they preach. This leaves much to be desired!

Some parents, for example, are great at teaching right behavior but not so good at following through in their own lives. In effect they tell their children, "Do as I say, not as I do." Children will understandably feel resentful when parents fail to live by the standards they preach. Children recognize the incongruence and may be disrespectful or rebellious when parents make demands.

On the other hand, parents who model right behavior but never provide explanations and good reasons for the values and beliefs they hold are also lacking appropriate skills. It is important that parents guide, equip, and empower their children by taking time to give the *whys* of the behaviors they expect from them. It's balance we're looking for, perhaps best described as a discipling role.

Discipling

The term *discipling* is derived from the root word *disciple*, which refers to one who leads or guides others. It is curious that while the concept of discipling is a popular one in the contemporary church, it is rarely used to refer to the task of parents training or guiding their own children. The terms *discipline* and *punishment* have mistakenly come to have similar meanings in our society. The question is whether parents should physically punish their children (by spanking or other means). Physical punishment is defended by some Christians by referring to "spare the rod and spoil the child" (see Prov. 13:24). However, it is important to consider how the rod was used by sheepherders in the pastoral culture of Old Testament times. It was an instrument to *guide* the sheep who needed direction because of ignorance, not as a means of beating them into submission.

Discipling is ideally built around a system of giving positive guidance to our children. Of the parenting styles presented earlier, authoritative parents influence their children by word and by deed, knowing how to supply an appropriate kind and amount of guidance.

The most effective way to discipline is by giving explanations, using reasoning, and, in general, encouraging a child's voluntary compliance. This has the advantage of avoiding a direct conflict of wills between parents and children.

Arcelia and Nate return home from their respective medical practices late one night to find their nanny asleep on the couch and their four-year-old daughter, Katrina, raiding the kitchen for chocolate cake. Arcelia tells Katrina it is too late for cake and that it's time for bed. Katrina refuses to go, saying that Roski, her stuffed dog, wants some cake first. Arcelia explains that cake has sugar, which will keep Roski awake, and that he'll probably even bark during the night and wake up the whole house. Katrina asks if milk is all right. Arcelia says she will warm her a little cup of milk.

Nate asks Katrina if she would like to pick a story and says he will read it to her in bed. She asks for the one with the big dinosaurs. Nate asks if that will scare her. Katrina tells him, "No, because Roski will protect me." All agree.

The authoritative parenting style best reflects the seven attributes of God's love. Parents who practice this style demonstrate care, responsiveness, giving, respect, knowing (understanding), forgiveness, and discipline. It is no wonder that children seem to thrive in the environment of high support and high control the authoritative parenting style provides.

Dual-earner parents have a unique opportunity to develop a parenting style that reflects the attributes of God's love. When you share the parenting role, you give each other the time and support necessary to be good-enough parents. You find ways to complement each other by relating to your children in your own ways. You both take clear leadership when it comes to nurturing and guiding your children. Sharing the parenting role, you provide positive guidance based on appropriate amounts of support and control that encourages your children to develop into mature, responsible persons. Working together, you can be good-enough parents, even with the pressures and demands of the dual-earner marriage.

13

Substitute Childcare
What Is Best for the Children?

Marge and Tim Robinson have invited Roberto and Teresea Flores and their two children together with Yvonne and David Porter and their three children over for a backyard cookout. It's been a hard week for each of these dual-earner couples. Now that supper is over and the kids are playing hide-and-seek, the three couples are taking a well-deserved rest in the warm summer evening. The topic of discussion turns to a common concern—how to best care for their children while they are at their jobs.

Marge begins by stating how guilty she feels about leaving two-year-old Daniel and four-year-old Lauri at a day-care center from 8 A.M. to 6 P.M. Monday through Friday. Roberto confesses that he is glad that he and Teresea can leave their children with his mother, who lives just five minutes away. Teresea agrees that she is grateful for Roberto's mother, but she has some disagreements with her method of discipline. Dave remarks that since he and Yvonne work at different times, they save a lot of money by each taking care of the children while the other works. Yvonne complains, however, that she and David spend very little time together from Monday to Friday.

This conversation is a reflection of what is the major difficulty encountered by dual-earner couples with children—finding a good solution for childcare needs. This is especially true when children are very young, but it can also be a major problem when a school-age child becomes ill. Dual-earner parents are frequently unsupported in their quest to find a caring and stimulating childcare environment and are deeply concerned, knowing that poor childcare can have a negative effect on the children, the family, and future generations.

The development of good substitute childcare can go a long way toward allowing both parents to work without their children suffering. But this is not enough! The workplace must begin to accommodate itself to the needs of working parents. The church and other institutions need to throw their weight behind dual-earner parents in encouraging businesses to create more family-friendly workplaces. The cost, not only to our children but to our society as a whole, is too great if we choose to do otherwise.

Ever since the advent of the industrial revolution, the family has been asked to accommodate itself to the economic institution. Most notably, parents have been asked to give their prime hours to working outside of the home. In return, the economic institution has made very few concessions to the needs of families.

The time has come to reverse this two-hundred-year trend. The cost has been too great. At present we have a generation of fathers who are trying to father but who have barely been fathered themselves. The future cost may be even greater to the children who come out of dual-earner homes. The next generation may struggle to parent while having barely been parented themselves. The care of children must come first! To require parents to give priority to work instead of caring for their children is tantamount to selling our children's birthright for a bowl of economic porridge.

As an ideal, all childcare would be done within the home, with a mother, father, grandparents, and a rich assortment of other caring and loving persons sharing childcare responsibilities. But this ideal is rarely possible, especially when both parents work outside of the home. Even though this arrangement can't often be duplicated, there are a wide range of alternative childcare strategies that can attempt to approximate this ideal. Before examining some possible options, we will examine some general characteristics that are important for evaluating any method of alternative childcare.

Characteristics of Good Alternative Childcare

Low Caregiver/Child Ratio

Obviously, the lower the caregiver to child ratio the better, and, of course, the lower the ratio the higher the cost of day care is likely to be. As a rule of thumb, a good day-care center should have a ratio of at least one teacher to every fifteen children for older children (over five years old). For younger children (under five years old), the need for more individual assistance and attention is greater, and therefore the ratio should be even lower.

There is some evidence that being cared for by someone other than parents can benefit a child. The experience of gaining confidence and support from someone other than parents can serve to break an unhealthy exclusive dependence on parents or caregivers. Also, for the only child, the experience in a day-care environment can help develop his or her social and interactive skills that will be necessary in order to get along with other children later in school. A day-care center with a low caregiver/child ratio is more likely to help a child develop these beneficial skills.

Number of Children in the Day-Care Center

Besides the importance of a low caregiver to child ratio, children do better in smaller day-care centers. Larger day-care centers tend to be less personal. It is also more likely that a hierarchical structure will emerge, making it less likely that a child will be able to establish an intimate, enduring relationship with one or more caregivers.

High Personal Contact with Caregiver

Caregivers can have different styles of working with children. The more personal their style—spending time in one-to-one interaction with a child—the better. Good caregivers will include nurturing in their contact with children.

Effective personal contact can also be based on an understanding of the background and family situation of each child. It is important that parents communicate to substitute caregivers anything that is happening in their lives that might be affecting the child, any difficulties the child may be experiencing with siblings, or any particular challenges in his or her current developmental stage.

Rich Verbal Stimulation

Besides meeting a child's need for nurturing, good caregivers will engage in rich verbal interaction with the child. This needs to go beyond the mere use of proper grammar to include the caregiver's ability to read and tell stories and attempts at stimulating the child's imagination.

Adequate Space

Children need an environment in which they can play creatively and explore. Cramped or crowded facilities will have an adverse effect on the social relationships between the children and also with their caregivers. Adequate space also includes a clean environment and ample play equipment. Whereas expensive toys are not crucial, there should be physical objects available that are both safe and challenging to children.

Knowledgeable Caregiver

Good caregivers will have a good working understanding of a child's developmental stages. They will have the insight to differentiate the normal developmental difficulties from more personal difficulties that have nothing to do with normal development. Ideally, this knowledge is gained both through personal experience in caring for children and through academic training. It is not necessary, however, that *all* workers have both, but someone in an official position should understand child development.

Compatible Moral and Value Systems

While it might not be necessary that substitute caregivers have identical religious beliefs as the child's parents, they should at least not be in conflict with the parents' values and beliefs. It is not uncommon for caregivers with strong religious convictions to try to teach their beliefs to the children they care for. When the caregiver's beliefs are the same as the parents', this might be desirable. However, when a caregiver is of another religious persuasion, parents need to communicate carefully their own beliefs and the important points they wish to see developed in their own children.

Much of what children learn is caught and not taught. Thus, it is also important that parents communicate to the caregiver the behaviors they wish for their children to develop. Parents who want to avoid such behaviors as eating junk food, watching soap operas, smoking, cursing, and so on, need to make sure that their child's caregiver is not modeling these behaviors.

Alternative Methods of Childcare

There are six major caregiving alternatives available to dual-earner parents: tag-team parenting, substitute childcare in the home, substitute care in someone else's home, neighborhood childcare centers, childcare facilities at work, and flexible schedules at work.

Tag-Team Parenting

This alternative consists of dual-earner parents taking turns doing all of the parenting themselves. Needless to say, this alternative is possible only for parents who do not both work at the same time. In marriages where work schedules can be arranged to accommodate childcare, children have the advantage of being parented by both their mother and father. The tag-team approach can be a very positive coparenting experience because children have the opportunity to bond equally with both parents, and both parents have the opportunity to participate in the lives of their children.

There are major drawbacks to the tag-team approach. Parents who work different shifts must also take alternate parenting shifts. Although both parents may spend quality time with their children, they may spend little *joint* quality time with their children. Parents need to relate to their children as a unit as well as individually. Some tag-team parents who split days and nights five days a week may find sufficient time for joint parenting activities on weekends. Even if they succeed in finding time to parent their children together, they may find that they have little time for their own relationship.

Substitute Childcare in the Home

Hiring a caregiver to watch children in the home can be an ideal arrangement, but it is usually very expensive and not affordable for many dual-earner parents.

Substitute childcare in the home works best when the caregiver is another adult also residing in the household. The most ideal situation, both financially and emotionally, is to have a widowed grandparent living in and caring for the children. Such an arrangement can financially and emotionally benefit both grandparents and parents. But even more importantly, such an arrangement can be an enormous social and emotional benefit for both grandchildren and grandparents. In most societies through history, it was the grandparents rather than the parents who transmitted values and beliefs to children. A weakness in the contemporary family is that many children have little opportunity to learn the important things of life from their grandparents. A resident grandparent can provide this opportunity, and in the process, the grandparent can benefit from rich emotional fulfillment.

A resident unmarried aunt, uncle, or other adult can also be a good source of substitute childcare in the home. In order for such resident childcare to work, however, parents must be very clear about social and emotional boundaries, which serve to protect relationships. Parents must take care to insure that a substitute caregiver does not become the parent. Clear boundaries will define expectations and responsibilities in such a way that a grandparent or aunt doesn't become a third parent. Children will need to know that when their mother and/or father is home, *they* are in charge, they are the real parents.

The important role of substitute childcare provided by a grandparent or other relative can best be performed when children are also in strong bonded relationships with their parents. Substitute caregiving must not mean substitute parenting.

Substitute Care in Someone Else's Home

Making arrangements for childcare in someone else's home has many advantages. A friend of ours takes her daughter to a trusted neighbor who has two daughters of her own. The three girls enjoy playing together and it is a warm, family environment that provides security and love.

Neighborhood Childcare Centers

A neighborhood childcare center is any place designed to provide care for children, usually associated with a church, school, government agency, or volunteer organization. Needless to say, the quality of neighborhood childcare centers varies greatly. Each of the criteria for evaluating childcare described earlier is especially applicable when evaluating a neighborhood childcare center.

The best neighborhood childcare centers are limited in size, have a positive caregiver to child ratio, and are staffed by emotionally mature persons who have an understanding of children and are dedicated to their social, emotional, and spiritual development.

Childcare Facilities at Work

The last two alternatives—utilizing childcare facilities at work and creating flexible work schedules—represent a yet underdeveloped source of childcare. These alternatives also require that businesses make some concession to the needs of dual-earner parents.

The good news for the 1990s is that, in response to the increased number of mothers who are now a part of the workforce, the business community has finally begun to accommodate itself to the needs of the family. Companies have been instituting family-friendly policies because they have found that it is in their own best interests to retain the services of valuable workers.

Some businesses provide company owned and operated childcare centers at the work site. For the most part, businesses have done this only on the basis of the bottom line, when they are convinced that it is an investment that will pay profitable dividends in the form of better employee performance. Where on-site childcare centers have been tried, the evidence supports the wisdom of such company investments.

In general, employees have been satisfied with the childcare given at work sites. In company childcare centers, parents can visit their children at breaks and lunchtime. This not only adds to the child's sense of security, but it also gives parents a greater sense of control over the quality of the center than they might have at a neighborhood facility where they do not have the opportunity to spend time with their children.

However, because of the expense, only large corporations have established childcare centers. Company childcare centers will probably not become available to parents who are employed by smaller businesses.

Flexible Work Schedules

Businesses might accommodate the needs of employed parents by building more flexibility into work schedules. This is especially true when there is little more than tradition to explain why a rigid 9 A.M. to 5 P.M. work schedule is maintained. Flexible work schedules take one of three forms: *flextime, flexplace,* and *flexload.*

Flextime refers to the practice of giving workers more flexible work schedules. In its simplest form, flextime offers a worker more control of his or her work schedule. It can also allow an employee more time off when needed for childbirth or when a child is sick. Arlie Hochschild states that only 2–3 percent of workers utilize flexible scheduling. She believes that the main reason employees do not take advantage of flextime is because it elicits envy from other workers and is often seen as a sign that one isn't serious about one's job. She also noted that in companies in which flextime is a possibility, line managers often look unfavorably at workers who request a flexible work schedule. Workers fear that a boss may not be as willing to recommend advancement or a salary increase to a person who requests time off for family reasons.[17]

Whereas the need for flextime is greatest among lower-income workers, the opportunity for it is greatest for those who earn more. Women in upper-salary positions often don't use flextime because they believe it will adversely affect their careers, so the women who are most likely to use flextime are those in middle-salaried positions. Women in lower-income positions are usually not offered flextime by businesses.

Flexplace refers to greater flexibility in the place at which work might be done. In his 1979 book *Future Shock*, Alvin Toffler argued that the electronic-computer revolution would someday make it possible for increasing numbers of persons to work out of their homes instead of at a central workplace.[18] There are few reasons why a person who is getting paid to work at a computer terminal can't do most of this work at home. Carol, a mother of school-aged children, spends her mornings at the computer and fax machine so she is available when her children come home at noon. Susan arranges for a baby-sitter to take her young children to the local park each day while she spends time on the phone for her self-employment. There are opportunities to find creative ways to combine the roles of work and parenting.

Parents who are fortunate to be employed by a company open to flexplace can work and take care of their children at the same time. But the advances of flexplace have been slow, causing us to question Toffler's optimistic prediction that the home would soon become the center of cottage industries.

Flexload refers to when a company is willing for an employee to alter the number of hours worked per week depending on childcare needs. Flexload is possible in work situations where it is not imperative that work be done immediately.

As a dual-earner parent, you need to be informed of your options so that you can make the best childcare arrangements possible. You must research childcare alternatives and be able to evaluate the existing facilities and options wisely. Then you can provide the intellectual, emotional, and spiritual best for your children and put the least strain on your family while maintaining your demanding dual-career schedule.

Part

6

Successful
Acrobatics

14

Doing It Well

Some dual-earners do it well! It is not easy, but these marriages and families manage not only to survive but to thrive within the time demands that result when both spouses work outside of the home.

One of the greatest pressures faced by dual-earner couples is balancing work and family life. The obvious sources of this pressure are overload and conflict due to the multiple roles each spouse must play. Couples who do it well have learned from experience that they need to develop multiple responses, resources, and strategies for balancing the increased responsibilities, demands, and pressures of the dual-earner marriage and family.

A Proactive Response

Chances are that, as a dual-earner, you feel you have little or no control over your own life. You may feel like you are being controlled by external circumstances and forces and that your only option is to react. In order to do it well, dual-earner couples need to develop a *proactive response* to both work and family life.

When you have a *reactive* response to circumstances, you merely respond to the pressures and tensions created by work and family life. Picture the movement of a group of balls on a pool table after they have been struck by the cue ball. The force of the cue ball sends all the other balls colliding off each other and off the sides of the pool table. In a reactive model, the persons or things (pool balls) simply make adjustments to pressures (cue ball) and while this is good, it is not good enough.

When you have a *proactive* response to circumstances, you take intentional steps toward controlling your life rather than merely reacting to external forces and pressures. You seek a new understanding or adopt a new posture toward your situation. When you have a proactive response, there is hope that you can be liberated from being controlled and can instead begin to assume control over the circumstances that are the source of tension and conflict.

Know What You Can't Change

A proactive response to the work/family balancing act begins with distinguishing between what you can change and what you can't. Start with the prayer of Reinhold Niebuhr: "God, give me serenity to accept what cannot be changed, courage to change what should be changed, and wisdom to distinguish the one from the other." If you find yourself in a situation you cannot change, then a proactive response begins with accepting this fact and doing the best you can under the circumstances.

When Jack took several years off from his university teaching to attend seminary, we had to accept a difficult situation. At that point in our marriage, our two children were three and four years old. Our meager savings were not enough to sustain us through those several years of seminary, so it was necessary that we both work part-time while Jack was going to school.

To save money we moved into a tiny apartment in a crowded housing complex in a low-income area. It was difficult to keep from getting on each other's nerves in our limited space, and the apartment walls were so thin that we had trouble sleeping through the blaring television or the arguments of the neighbors next door. We could do little about our situation, but once we accepted this, we took comfort in the fact that life would be better when Jack returned to full-time teaching.

Identifying Resources

You may feel trapped in a situation in which there actually are some constructive actions you can take. The second step in a proactive approach is to identify existing and potential resources. A resource is anything that can be of potential value to you or your family in your present situation. A resource can take a variety of forms—financial, material, psychological, social, cultural. You may have valuable resources you are not presently using because you are not aware of them.

For example, your own children may be capable of taking responsibility for many more of the household tasks than you are presently asking them to do. Our children were eight and nine years old when Judy began a full-time family therapy practice. In preparation for becoming a truly dual-earner family, we taught our children to take more responsibility for their lives at home. We were amazed at how quickly Jacque and Jeff learned and even took pride in making their own beds, putting away their own clothes and toys, cleaning their own rooms, and doing household tasks such as taking out the garbage. They even asked if they could do *more* household tasks for pay.

Friends and neighbors can also be a rich, untapped resource. It may be the case that "you have not because you ask not." Self-sufficiency in modern society is like a social disease—people come to believe that they must not rely on anyone else. This is in sharp contrast to the mutual interdependence found in traditional societies where people are integrated into caring and supportive interlocking communities.

You may not have extended family members living near you, but you may have friends who can be drawn into a tighter support network for you and your children. Although we tried to use tag-team parenting (see chapter 13), there were times when work commitments prevented both of us from being home with our children when they came home from school. Our answer was to ask a retired couple who lived across the street to watch our children on such occasions. This couple had grandchildren of their own, but they lived hundreds of miles away. Our children had grandparents, but they lived thousands of miles away. This couple became like a grandma and grandpa to our children. They proved to be a rich resource for us as a family, and we believe our children enriched their lives as well.

You may also have unrecognized resources at your workplace. Recent evidence indicates that when business corporations offer family support facilities such as day-care centers to workers, the centers are underutilized. Businesses will be responsive to the needs of their workers when they are convinced that providing day-care facilities, flextime, and other arrangements that benefit families will be financially profitable. Working mothers and fathers may too often fail to make their needs known to their employers. It is important to remember that your working environment is a potential place to develop resources.

The Balancing Act: Work and Family Life

We are enraptured as we witness a professional juggler keeping an assortment of objects up in the air. To learn this skill, jugglers must spend much time and effort perfecting their art.

Living in a dual-earner family is much like juggling, and dual-earner couples need to be willing to devote time and effort to practicing the fine art of balancing work and family life. Much of the necessary balancing involves maintaining boundaries around our work and around our family life in order to prevent each from negatively affecting the other.

For good or ill, work and family life can mutually affect each other in a number of ways. Our performance at work is affected by what is happening in our family life. The quality of our family life is, in turn, affected by our work. Those who study the relationship between work and family have coined the term *spillover* to refer to the negative or unhealthy ways in which these two important areas of our lives affect each other.[19]

There are four major areas in family life where spillover from work occurs—marriage, relationships with children, leisure, and home management. Spillover may also occur from family to work. Dual-earners who successfully do it well develop strategies to avoid any disruptive spillover.

Work-to-Marriage Spillover

Even in single-earner marriages, partners often complain about the intrusiveness of their jobs outside the home. While the spillover from work in the dual-earner marriage is at least double that of the single-earner marriage, the magnitude of the effect is more likely to create multiple areas of spillover.

Take a moment as a couple to respond to the following four statements as a way of helping you and your spouse understand how much work-to-marriage spillover occurs in your family. With each spouse answering separately, circle the answer that best represents your feelings about each statement: 1 = strongly disagree, 2 = disagree, 3 = neutral, 4 = agree, 5 = strongly agree.

Work-to-Marriage Spillover

	strongly disagree	disagree	neutral	agree	strongly agree
1. My job keeps me from spending time with my spouse.	1	2	3	4	5
2. Worrying about my job is interfering with my relationship with my spouse.	1	2	3	4	5
3. After work I am often too tired to do things with my spouse.	1	2	3	4	5
4. My marriage suffers because of my work.	1	2	3	4	5

Add up your responses to statements one through four to obtain your total score. A score of sixteen to twenty indicates that there is considerable spillover from your work to your marriage. Compare your total score with your spouse's, noting the degree of similarity or difference between your two scores. Also note the statements on which the two of you differ by at least two points. Discuss ways in which you and/or your spouse can decrease the amount of spillover from work.

Work-to-Relationships-with-Children Spillover

The major barrier to being a good-enough parent in a dual-earner household is the time that both parents must devote to work. The following four statements are designed as a way of helping you and your spouse understand the extent to which your work spills over into your relationships with your children. Again, circle the answer that best represents your feelings about each statement.

Work-to-Relationships-with-Children Spillover

	strongly disagree	disagree	neutral	agree	strongly agree
1. My job makes it hard for me to have a good relationship with my children.	1	2	3	4	5
2. My working hours interfere with the amount of time I spend with my children.	1	2	3	4	5
3. Because I am often irritable after work, I am not as good a parent as I would like to be.	1	2	3	4	5
4. When I get home from work, I often do not have the energy to be a good parent.	1	2	3	4	5

Again, add your responses to the four statements to obtain your total score. A score of sixteen to twenty is an indication that there is considerable spillover from your work to your relationships with your children. Compare your answers with your spouse and discuss ways in which you and/or your spouse can guard against your work interfering with your relationships with your children.

Work-to-Leisure Spillover

When a working wife with four school-age children was asked about her leisure time, she replied, "Leisure, what's that?" One of the first things to go in dual-earner marriages is quality leisure time. Below are four statements that can help you reflect on the spillover from your work to your leisure activities. Respond to each statement as you have for the preceding exercises.

Work-to-Leisure Spillover

	strongly disagree	disagree	neutral	agree	strongly agree
1. My job makes it difficult to enjoy my free time outside of work.	1	2	3	4	5
2. The amount of time I spend working interferes with how much free time I have.	1	2	3	4	5
3. Worrying about my job makes it hard for me to enjoy myself outside of work.	1	2	3	4	5
4. Because I am often tired after work, I don't see friends as much as I would like.	1	2	3	4	5

After you have totaled your scores, compare them with your spouse's and discuss ways in which you can build more quality leisure time into your marriage.

Work-to-Home-Management Spillover

Many dual-earner couples encounter frustration and conflict over doing housework and must be adaptable and flexible in the strategies they use to get it done. Responding to the following statements will help you identify the degree to which work hinders your attempts to manage your household affairs.

Work-to-Home-Management Spillover

	strongly disagree	disagree	neutral	agree	strongly agree
1. My job makes it difficult for me to get household chores done.	1	2	3	4	5
2. I spend so much time working that I am unable to get much done at home.	1	2	3	4	5
3. Worrying about my job interferes with my ability to get things done around the house.	1	2	3	4	5
4. When I get home from my job, I do not have the energy to do work around the house.	1	2	3	4	5

After you have totaled your scores, compare them with your spouse's and discuss ways in which you can together better manage what needs to be done in your home.

Family-to-Work Spillover

If you are like most dual-earner couples, you are more frustrated by work-to-family than you are by family-to-work spillover. However, you also know that spillover from the family to work can have very disruptive consequences in your personal and family life. When you are hindered from doing good work at your job, you may be deprived of the financial and emotional resources you need to reinvest yourself in your family life.

Following are seven sentence-completion statements that can help you get in touch with family-to-work spillover. Simply complete each of these statements.

1. If my child doesn't want me to work, when I go to work

   _____
   _____
   _____.

2. If one of my children is home sick, when I go to work

   _____
   _____
   _____.

3. If my family doesn't want me to work overtime, when I go to work

   _____
   _____
   _____.

4. If my children respect my job, when I get to work

   _____

_____

_____.

5. If my home life is satisfying, when I get to work

_____

_____

_____.

6. If I have a problem at home, when I get to work

_____

_____

_____.

7. I work best when

_____

_____

_____.

Share and compare with your spouse how each of you completed the above sentences. Focus on the statements that most directly reflect the spillover issues in your family. You may also wish to share your answers with your children. They need to know of the struggles you experience when you are needed both at home and at work. They also need to be aware of your needs and how they can help you do all that you must do.

Alternative Ways of Balancing Work and Family Life

Although all dual-earner marriages have much in common, each is significantly different as well. There is no one way to successfully (and sanely) balance work and family life. Spouses can work together to creatively generate your own alternatives for balancing work and family life.

The figure below shows alternative ways in which husbands and wives might attempt to balance work and family life. Since each spouse may have a differing level of commitment to work and home, the figure represents levels of commitment on a continuum. The vertical axis on the table is the continuum *commitment to work,* and the horizontal axis is *commitment to family.* Within these levels of commitment appear four different strategies spouses use to balance work and family life—*adversaries, acrobats, allies,* or *accommodators.*[20]

Adversaries

In marriages in which both partners have a high commitment to their work and a low commitment to their

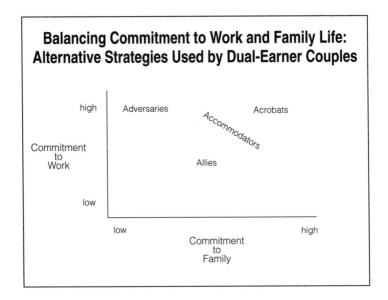

home, spouses can be described as *adversaries* (top left side of figure). Partners who are adversaries experience a failed attempt to balance concern for work and family. They may say they value home life as much as work, but not enough to give up their high commitment to work. Neither spouse is willing to take responsibility for the home; instead each hopes the other will do so. As a result, they exist in an adversarial relationship. One unfortunate consequence of an adversarial relationship is that family life suffers from a lack of attention.

"I don't have time to talk about it today," Frank said while brushing by Martha with a kiss, hugging Mindy and Retha, Mindy's pink teddy bear, wrestling a hand free from his briefcase and overcoat, and grabbing his sack lunch from the countertop. "You'll pick up Mindy from day care?" fled from Martha's lips as the door banged shut. She knew that, once again, the day would revolve around who was to pick up Mindy, who had agreed to what, who was supposed to be responsible, who was to blame. It seemed that a vicious circle was forming around their beloved child, who, feeling the effects of her parents' strain, was acting out in day care—using curse words, even hitting other children.

Martha would try to reach Frank all day once again, but he would be in meetings, or he would call her and she would be showing a house. Were she to reach him, he would say that he thought it was her turn and besides, he had an important meeting. He'd promise to do it next time. Then he would have to go. Before she had a chance to finish her first cup of coffee, the day was already decided and her fate with it. She was a married person competing with the man she loved over whose job was more important. She felt all alone as she held Mindy and Retha. Such is life when dual-earner partners become adversaries.

Acrobats

Marriage partners who both have a high commitment to their work and their home life can be described as *acrobats* (top right corner of figure). While these couples are able to successfully meet the demands in both the work and home arenas, they need the agility of an acrobat. Acrobats will most likely experience conflict while trying to do it all.

Kenny, an accountant, had always wanted a garage where he could keep tools and fix things. He hadn't really known what he would fix, not having grown up fixing things, but he knew that he could do it if he gave himself a chance. He hoped that he could share time in the garage workshop with his children.

Kenny's wife, Sue, felt convinced that her children would benefit from time spent in the creative arts. Lessons were available in almost anything these days. She thought that her appreciation of music and drama would rub off on them in tangible, participatory ways. She looked forward to helping them practice and watching their performances.

Sue's desires had even borne fruit in her own career as she had recently become the assistant director of the local repertory theater. The theater offered classes for all ages, and Kenny soon found that rather than spending time with him in his workshop, the children's free time was completely absorbed by Sue's theater programs. Not only that, Sue's professional role often forced Kenny to be the one to sacrifice his evenings to pick up the children and take care of their evening meals, study time, and bedtime rituals. Even that time was cut short by his career advancement and the increasingly larger accounting projects he had to complete. Sue also found less and less time to enjoy the children because the children had classes during her free time, and when they were out of class, she had to run off to a performance.

Scheduled around the clock and around the children, Kenny and Sue rarely had time to speak at length with each other. Their acrobatics put them in danger of serving only events and demands, rather than serving one another in love.

Allies

Couples who are *allies* are represented in the very center of the figure. In these marriages, both spouses are together in their degree of commitment to their jobs and their home. They are allies in the sense that neither expects the other to carry more of the load in the home. While they truly share responsibility for family life, they also strive to be equal in their commitment to their jobs. As allies, neither spouse needs to carry the entire load of either earning a living or managing the home.

"Nevin, I've got a parent/teacher meeting Thursday. Could you get the kids and do dinner?" Amanda had been so busy with lesson plans and coaching volleyball that Nevin was happy to ease her tensions. She had pulled extra weight in the home last month when Nevin had had to put in a lot of overtime preparing a presentation to attract an important new client.

Nevin and Amanda thought of themselves as allies. While both had demanding careers—Nevin was an advertising executive and Amanda a junior high school teacher and volleyball coach—they encouraged and assisted each other as they pursued the careers they loved. One would often pitch in to help the other, editing each other's presentations, running errands, cooking and serving dinner for unexpected guests, such as

Amanda's volleyball team or Nevin's clients. Both contributed financially to the family's bills and savings in equitable percentages.

Accommodators

Accommodators agree to be different. In an accommodating marriage, one spouse gives priority commitment to his or her job, the other to the home. Accommodators choose to balance work and home life through complementarity. As a result, this strategy for balancing work and family life can't be represented in one place within the figure; it can work well in a variety of circumstances.

While allies stress equality in contributing to work and home life, accommodators find that complementary roles accomplish the same thing in a different way. Accommodators in a complementary marriage benefit from the individual strengths of each spouse rather than seeking to duplicate the skills of either. It may be easier for one spouse to assume more responsibility for home life than the other for a variety of reasons—one spouse may have a more flexible work schedule, a workplace closer to home, or work status carrying with it the authority to take off work when desired. The accommodator style may also take advantage of differences between partners in their personal skills and strengths as providers, parents, and homemakers.

There are two subtypes of accommodator marriages: the *traditional accommodating marriage* and the *reversal accommodating marriage.* In the traditional accommodating marriage, the husband gives higher commitment to his job and the wife to the home. Due to a variety of circumstances, reversal accommodation has emerged as a new type of marriage in which the husband has a stronger commitment to the home and the wife a stronger commitment to her job.

As two-year-old Jenny awoke, she cried, probably meaning that she was ready to get up from her nap. Randall put down his paint brush and stepped quickly away from the easel. He would first go get Jenny, hold her and reassure her; then he would fix her a little snack.

For the first year of Jenny's life, Paula stayed home and worked part-time. As her education and skills became apparent at work, Paula was offered a high-level administrative position. She and Randall decided that they would be better off if she took the job and Randall resigned from his full-time title research job. This would give him time to spend with Jenny and return to something he was trained in and loved—art. Paula's new full-time salary would be more than Randall's full-time salary and her part-time salary combined, and this would give Randall the opportunity to paint.

Paula and Randall enjoyed the role reversal their accommodators' style afforded them as they each flourished. Paula received accolades and an early promotion at work. Randall's art was shown in a number of office settings and began to sell. Although it was clear that Paula was the primary provider, they were comfortable with the arrangement. They enjoyed their usual social commitments and maintained a wide circle of friends.

Growing Together

Couples who do it well have learned from experience to balance the increased responsibilities, demands, and pressures of the dual-earner marriage and family. Instead of merely reacting to the pressures and tensions created by work and family life, you can adopt a proactive response, knowing what you can and can't change and identifying existing and potential resources to help you ease the pressure your multiple roles create. You can learn to recognize where spillover from work is affecting your marriage and family in negative, unhealthy, or disruptive ways. And you can learn the fine art of juggling—finding alternative ways to balance work and family life to everyone's advantage.

Balancing work and family life in your demanding, dual-earner marriage does not mean you have to do everything perfectly. The juggling act takes concentration, wise discernment, and practice. You simply strive to be good enough so you don't continually drop the balls.

Couples who are good-enough jugglers try and fail and try again. You try and fail and try again to resolve your conflicts in healthy ways that bring new growth and renewed intimacy into the relationship. You try and fail and try again to establish and come back to the foundations for a strong and growing marriage. You try and fail and try again to sort out, create, and adjust to new roles. When pressures threaten to pull your marriage apart, you pull together and intentionally recreate the bonds between you. And in the process of working together to balance the multiple challenges and demands of your dual-earner marriage, you will find that you have deepened your intimacy, rekindled your sexual passion, and created a shared meaning for your lives together that carries beyond you into family, into work, and into the world. Putting forth your best efforts allows you to grow together rather than grow apart, and it keeps you centered on what God has ordained as the one-flesh meaning of your dual-earner lives.

Notes

1. The ideas for the dual-earner marriage role titles are taken from Jean Potuchek, "Employed Wives' Orientations to Breadwinning: A Gender Theory Analysis," *Journal of Marriage and the Family* 54 (1992): 548–58.

2. Ibid.

3. Arlie Hochschild, "Beyond the Second Shift: Denying Needs at Home or Contesting Rules at Work?" Verbal presentation given at the annual meeting of the National Council on Family Relations, Orlando, Florida, November 8, 1992.

4. Ibid.

5. Patricia Ulbrich, "The Determinants of Depression in Two-Income Marriages," *Journal of Marriage and the Family* 50 (1988): 121–31.

6. Linda Nyquist et al., "Household Responsibilities in Middle-class Couples: The Contribution of Demographic and Personality Variables," *Sex Roles* 12 (1985): 15–34.

7. Lucia Gilbert, *Men in Dual-Career Families: Current Realities and Future Prospects* (Hillsdale, N.J.: Lawrence Erlbaum Publishers, 1985), 114.

8. John Rosemond, "The 'Nest' Is Empty at Long Last," *Charlotte Observer,* April 16, 1991, 8.

9. Sheila Hite, *The Hite Report* (New York: Macmillan, 1976).

10. Diana Ehrensaft, *Parenting Together: Men and Women Sharing the Care of Their Children* (Chicago: University of Illinois Press, 1990).

11. Ibid.

12. See especially chapter 1, "Fathers and Child Development: An Integrative Overview," by Michael Lamb, and chapter 11, "The Role of the Father in Cognitive, Academic, and Intellectual Development," by Norma Radin, in *The Role of the Family in Child Development* (edited by Michael Lamb, [New York: John Wiley and Sons, 1981]).

13. Myron Chartier, "Parenting: A Theological Model," *Journal of Psychology and Theology* 6 (1978): 54–61.

14. See Diane Baumrind, "Parental Disciplinary Patterns and Social Competence in Children," *Youth and Society* 9 (1978): 239–76; and Boyd Rollins and Darwin Thomas, "Parental Support, Power, and Control Techniques in the Socialization of Children," in *Contemporary Theories About the Family: Volume 1* (edited by Wesley Burr, Reuben Hill, Inan Nye, and Ira Reiss [New York: The Free Press, 1979], 317–64.

15. Christopher Lasch, *Haven in a Heartless World: The Family Besieged* (New York: Basic, 1977), 167–98.

16. For a summary of 235 research studies on the topic see Boyd Rollins and Darwin Thomas, "Parental Support, Power, and Control Techniques in the Socialization of Children," in *Contemporary Theories About the Family: Volume 1* (edited by Wesley Burr, Reuben Hill, Inan Nye, and Ira Reiss [New York: The Free Press, 1979], 317–64).

17. Hochschild, "Beyond the Second Shift."

18. Alvin Toffler, *Future Shock* (New York: Random, 1970).

19. The statements contained in the following scales *(Work-to-Marriage Spillover, Work-to-Relationships-with-Children Spillover,* and *Work-to-Leisure Spillover)* are taken from Stephen Small and Dave Riley's article "Toward a Multidimensional Assessment of

Work Spillover into Family Life," *Journal of Marriage and the Family* 52 (February 1990): 51–61. The statements referring to *Family-to-Work Spillover* that follow are taken from Stephen F. Duncan, "The Balancing Act: Balancing Work and Family Life," Circular HE-632 Auburn University, Ala.: Alabama Cooperative Extension Service, n.d.

20. We have taken these topologies from "Stress and the Two-Career Couple," by D. T. Hall and F. S. Hall, in *Current Concerns in Occupational Stress* (edited by C. L. Cooper and R. Payne [New York: John Wiley, 1980], 243–66).

Bibliography

Armin, R. "A Practice Model for Reconciling Role Incompatibilities in the Family-Occupational Role System." Paper presented at the annual meeting of the National Council on Family Relations, Orlando, Fla., 1992.

Balswick, Jack, and Judith Balswick. "Adam and Eve in America." *Christianity Today* 34, no. 4 (16 July 1990): 15–18.

Barnett, R., N. Marshall, and J. Pleck. "Men's Multiple Roles and Their Relationship to Men's Psychological Distress." *Journal of Marriage and the Family* 54 (1992): 358–67.

Baumrind, Diane. "Parental Disciplinary Patterns and Social Competence in Children." *Youth and Society* 9 (1978): 239–76.

Berry, J. "Stress and Child Responsibilities for Fathers in Dual-Earner Families." Paper presented at the annual meeting of the National Council on Family Relations, Orlando, Fla., 1992.

Bower, S., and A. Davis. "Work Shift and Child Care Arrangements: Family Correlates." Paper presented at the annual meeting of the National Council on Family Relations, Orlando, Fla., 1992.

Chartier, Myron. "Parenting: A Theological Model." *Journal of Psychology and Theology* 6 (1978): 54–61.

Cherpas, C. "Dual-Career Families: Terminology, Typologies, and Work and Family Issues." *Journal of Counseling and Development* 63 (1984): 616–20.

Coltrane, S., and M. Ishii-Kuntz. "Men's Housework: A Life Course Perspective." *Journal of Marriage and the Family* 54 (1992): 43–57.

Darling-Fisher, C., and L. Tiedje. "The Impact of Maternal Employment Characteristics on Fathers' Participation in Child Care." *Family Relations* 39 (1990): 20–26.

Duncan, S. "The Balancing Act: Balancing Work and Family Life." HE-632 Auburn University, Ala.: Alabama Cooperative Extension Service, n.d.

Ehrensaft, Diana. *Parenting Together: Men and Women Sharing the Care of Their Children.* Chicago: University of Illinois Press, 1990.

Fisher, J., and D. Sollie. "Married with Children: A Prospective Study of Dual Career or Husband Career Lifestyle." Paper presented at the annual meeting of the National Council on Family Relations, Orlando, Fla., 1992.

Gilbert, L. *Men in Dual-Career Families: Current Realities and Future Prospects.* Hillsdale, N.J.: Erlbaum, 1985.

Grimm, K., C. Huddeston, and M. Perry-Jenkins. "Work Conditions, Self-Esteem and Parents' Perceptions of Parenting in Dual-Earner Families." Paper presented at the annual meeting of the National Council on Family Relations, Orlando, Fla., 1992.

Guelzow, M., G. Bird, and E. Koball. "An Exploratory Path Analysis of the Stress Process for Dual-Career Men and Women." *Journal of Marriage and the Family* 53 (1991): 151–64.

Hall, D. T., and F. S. Hall, in *Current Concerns in Occupational Stress,* C. L. Cooper and R. Payne, editors. New York: John Wiley, 1980.

Hanson, S., and T. Ooms. "The Economic Costs and Rewards of Two-Earner, Two-Parent Families." *Journal of Marriage and the Family* 53 (1991): 622–34.

Hawkins, A., and K. Woodworth. "Preparing Young Adults for the 'Second Shift.'" Paper presented at the annual meeting of the National Council on Family Relations, Orlando, Fla., 1992.

Hill, E., and B. Mill. "Who Is Responsible for What at Home?: The Division of Responsibility for Household Labor As Reported by Corporate Employees." Paper presented at the National Council on Family Relations, Orlando, Fla., 1992.

Hite, S. *The Hite Report.* New York: Macmillan, 1976.

Hochschild, Arlie. *The Second Shift: Working Parents and the Revolution at Home.* New York: Viking, 1989.

Holt, H., I. Thaulow, and I. Maerkedahl. "Do Working Time Arrangements Affect Stress and Welfare in the Family?" Paper presented at the annual meeting of the National Council on Family Relations, Orlando, Fla., 1992.

Hughes, D., and E. Galinsky. "Balancing Work and Family Life: Research and Corporate Application." In *Maternal Employment and Children's Development: Longitudinal Research,* edited by A. W. Gottfried and A. E. Gottfried. New York: Plenum, 1988, 233–68.

Keith, P., and R. Schafer. "Relative Deprivation, Equity/Inequity, and Psychological Well-Being: Men and Women in One- and Two-Job Families." *Journal of Family Issues* 8 (1987): 199–211.

Kennedy, G. "The Value and Commitment to Work and Family Roles: Influence of Gender and Family Background." Paper presented at the annual meeting of the National Council on Family Relations, Orlando, Fla., 1992.

Lasch, Christopher. *Haven in a Heartless World: The Family Besieged.* New York: Basic, 1977.

Lewis, S., and C. Cooper. "Stress in Two-Earner Couples and Stage in the Life-Cycle." *Journal of Occupational Psychology* 60 (1987): 289–303.

Lewis, S., D. Izraeli, and H. Hootsmans. *Dual-Earner Families: International Perspectives.* Newbury Park, Calif.: Sage, 1992.

Mattox, W. "The Family Friendly Corporation: Strengthening the Ties That Bind." *Family Policy* 5, no. 4 (November 1992): 1–11.

Maret, Elizabeth, and Barbara Finlay. "The Distribution of Household Labor among Women in Dual-Earner Marriages." *Journal of Marriage and the Family* 46 (1984): 357–64.

Nyquist et al. "Household Responsibilities in Middle-class Couples: The Contribution of Demographic and Personality Variables," *Sex Roles* 12 (1985): 15–34.

Oden, Thomas. *Game Free: A Guide to the Meaning of Intimacy.* New York: Harper and Row, 1974.

Perry-Jinkins, M. "Future Directions for Research on Dual-Earner Families: A Young Professional's Perspective." *Family Relations* 37 (1988): 226–28.

Peterson, R., and K. Gerson. "Determinants of Responsibility for Child Care Arrangements among Dual-Earner Couples." *Journal of Marriage and the Family* 54 (1992): 527–36.

Piotrkowski, C. *Work and the Family System: A Naturalistic Study of Working-Class and Lower-Middle-Class Families.* New York: Collier Macmillan, 1978.

Potuchek, J. "Employed Wives' Orientations to Breadwinning: A Gender Theory Analysis." *Journal of Marriage and the Family* 54 (1992): 548–58.

Presser, H. "Shift Work and Child Care among Young Dual-Earner American Parents." *Journal of Marriage and the Family* 50 (1988): 133–48.

Rice, D. *Dual-Career Marriage.* New York: Free Press, 1979.

Robert, T., A. Hawkins, and C. Marshall. "A Multi-Method Evaluation of a Program to Help Dual-Earner Couples Share Housework and Child Care." Paper presented at the annual meeting of the National Council on Family Relations, Orlando, Fla., 1992.

Rollins, Boyd, and Darwin Thomas, "Parental Support, Power, and Control Techniques in the Socialization of Children." In *Contemporary Theories About the Family: Volume 1,* edited by Wesley Burr, Reuben Hill, Inan Nye, and Ira Reiss. New York: Free Press, 1979, 317–64.

Rosemond, John. "The 'Nest' Is Empty at Long Last." *Charlotte Observer* April 16, 1991, 8.

Schnittger, M., and G. Bird. "Coping among Dual-Career Men and Women across the Family Life Cycle." *Family Relations* 39 (1990): 199–205.

Sexton, C., and D. Perlman. "Couples' Career Orientation, Gender Role Orientation, and Perceived Equity As Determinants of Marital Power." *Journal of Marriage and the Family* 51 (1989): 933–42.

Small, Stephen, and Dave Riley. "Toward a Multidimensional Assessment of Work Spillover into Family Life." *Journal of Marriage and the Family* 52 (February 1990): 51–61.

Stanley, S., J. Hunt, and L. Hunt. "The Relative Deprivation of Husbands in Dual-Earner Households." *Journal of Family Issues* 7 (1986): 3–20.

Toffler, Alvin. *Future Shock.* New York: Random, 1970.

Ulbrich, P. "The Determinants of Depression in Two-Income Marriages." *Journal of Marriage and the Family* 50 (1988): 121–31.